Will Payne

The Money Captain

Will Payne

The Money Captain

ISBN/EAN: 9783744724975

Printed in Europe, USA, Canada, Australia, Japan

Cover: Foto ©Thomas Meinert / pixelio.de

More available books at **www.hansebooks.com**

THE
MONEY CAPTAIN

BY

WILL PAYNE

AUTHOR OF "JERRY, THE DREAMER"

HERBERT S. STONE & COMPANY
CHICAGO & NEW YORK
MDCCCXCVIII

The Money Captain

CHAPTER I

FAR at the eastern edge of the marshy, rankly green prairie an enormous blotch of smoke hung in the brilliant horizon. Against it, low toward the earth, the slender pipes and chimneys of the steel works were faintly etched.

It was the first large sign of the city, and it spurred Nidstrom's impatience. The train was late and that last slow hour hurt his nerves.

He sat in one of the hard, revolving chairs in the smoking-car, next the window. His stout legs were stretched to the chair in front of him. His elbow rested on the window sill, careless of the dust and cinders, and he stared blankly at that marshy landscape. A straw hat was tilted to the back of his big head, disclosing the thinness of his yellowish hair, of silken fineness. The hat was in the current mode, and above that extremely broad, dome-like brow it had an effect of trivialness. His suit was of modest gray, presentable enough, and he wore tan shoes, a striped, limp shirt, a stiff standing collar and a bow tie. Nevertheless the critical in those matters would by no means have called him well-dressed. The tie was evidently a ready-made bow, and it was a little frayed at the upper edge. The standing rim of the collar was at least a half-inch too low, and the inch and a half that it lacked of meeting in front confessed an epoch which, to the careful young man of the spring of '97, would have seemed as good as antediluvian. There was everywhere a suggestion of the economical hardihood which aims merely at passing muster in the cheapest and easiest way. Nidstrom's face was broad and even heavy, with a wide mouth, flat nose, bulging brows and large contemplative eyes, light blue in color. The slow, grave, contemplative, almost bovine movement of his eyes had no reference at all, or only the slightest and most incidental, to the dispersed and ragged suburban panorama that was wheeling into view from the car window.

The Michigan city whence he came after

an over-Sunday reunion with his wife and baby had been tiny to his eyes, focused to Chicago's largeness, and dead to his ears, attuned to this Babel ahead; but its trees and grass and the creeping water of its little river had yielded themselves to him with a gracious intimacy that he could not get out of Washington Park. From the tyrannous thing ahead—the vast smoky jangling city, the innumerable stretches of grimy streets shaking with traffic, the endless iteration of dingy brick and stone—his mind turned back to that fragrant peace with a hunger that was partly nostalgia, and partly from his bad conscience.

Because to stand before Nell and tell her that he had ventured their little capital in a speculation in Consolidated Gas shares, and had lost it; to explain fumblingly that he had thought it was going to turn out differently— this, as it came to his wincing imagination at intervals with piercing vividness, seemed to him not very different from having to explain that he had mixed arsenic in the baby's milk for experimental purposes, with unfortunate and irretrievable results. At least, he should have told Nell all about the speculation. He wondered at himself with abjectness for not having told her. Then, again, he saw that he must not tell her; that to tell her would be only to get the burden of anxiety off his shoulders and upon her shoulders, to put up a provisional defense for himself at the expense of her peace. He came back to his doggedness. It had seemed a promising opportunity. He had done his best. The Fates must do the rest. And, after all, no doubt it still promised; no doubt he would win.

He looked at his watch. It was after ten o'clock. The Stock Exchange was open. For some thirty excruciating seconds it seemed a kind of fundamental failure of all boasted advances in the science of living that a man should be twelve miles from the Twelfth Street station at twelve minutes after ten without having any way of getting the last quotation on Consolidated Gas.

Ah, well, surely these three lumbering Swedes with tin dinner-pails in their hands, for whom the train had stopped, wouldn't know the quotation.

It was half-past ten when he jumped from the street car at the corner of Jackson Boulevard under the shadowing pillars and girders of the elevated road that stretched up Wabash Avenue like a huge superterrene tunnel. He faced west, in which direction the buildings grew taller. The mismated halves of the Great Northern towered four-

THE MONEY CAPTAIN

teen and sixteen stories at his right hand, and to the left loomed the dismal and vast façade of the Monadnock, like the gigantic projection of a mud fence. Taking to the roadway to avoid crossing the street, and dodging the cabs and bicycles, Nidstrom skirted the fenced excavation, a large square in extent, where the foundations of the new Postoffice were in course of preparation. Far below the street level, in the enormous clayey pit, steam engines hissed and pile drivers struck grunting blows. There floated faintly up to the clatter and clangor of the street the cries of teamsters and overseers as a hundred men toiled at the muddy beginnings of the great structure. Nidstrom kept on by the clean and glistening granite walls of the bank to that famous heart of business where the dumpy bulk of the Board of Trade blocks La Salle street.

At first glance the neighborhood had the effect of a thicket of huge buildings. Towering cornices rose everywhere, and the air about them was murky as though exhaled from the battle always waging there. At Nidstrom's back, across the street, the great two-story windows of the Board's trading room were open, and the cries of the brokers in the pits came out in a kind of striving roar. The wide stone flaggings, hot on the western side under the nearly vertical rays of the August sun, were thronged with people, all hurrying. Two policemen stood at the street joining and directed the endless flow of carts, vans and carriages, all behindhand and trying to catch up. Only the procession of the bank's tall granite pillars could afford to take time for dignity.

Brass signs beside the doorways and gilt lettering on the windows gave the names of banking and brokerage houses. The dominating note of the street was the swift, imperious, metallic click of the telegraph key. It played the tune to which the street marched. The pace was fast, but for the most part the army was good-natured.

A very pursy man, with a long, limp, red mustache, in a jaunty straw hat and an expansive suit of white flannel, popped from a cab and hastened up the steps of the bank. Wheat had advanced three cents over night and was advancing more. There were some calls for margins in his office. The big clock below the Board of Trade's amputated tower was ticking away his last twenty minutes. A gentleman of military bearing, the author of one of the calls, stepped from the bank door. The pursy man grinned.

"It's hell, ain't it!" he called in cheerful

THE MONEY CAPTAIN

and impersonal recognition of the exigencies of the situation, as he hastened by the military one—who might have his financial scalp before noon—and dove through the bank door.

Nidstrom went on to the arched entrance of the Cyclops Building, which was like the mouth of a tunnel piercing the base of a tall cliff, and pushed through one of a dozen doors whose hinges never rested from ten o'clock to four. In the mosaic-floored, glass-roofed court, he entered a small solid door bearing the sign: "Maxmann & Gregg."

The room was, perhaps, twenty feet square. The glazed upper sashes of the windows giving into the court were pulled down and the air was full of the low, swift humming of electrical fans. A big blackboard covered the north wall of the room. In a column at the left-hand end of it appeared the names of stocks, and long parallel lines of chalked figures gave the quotations. A step-ladder mounted on rollers stood before the board. A boy with a stick of chalk in one hand and a strip of paper, torn from the ticker, in the other, pushed the ladder back and forth and ran up and down it, marking in the figures from the paper. Between the windows was a similar blackboard, but smaller, where the quotations made on the local exchange were given, and the board on the south wall displayed the fluctuations in grain and provisions, telegraphed from the Board of Trade. On a table in the center of the room were files of telegrams, which were added to from moment to moment by an office boy. Next the door stood an upright box of polished wood, like a coffin on end, with a curving glass top out of which unwound a broad strip of white paper whereon the machinery within printed continuously paragraphs of news relating to the different markets.

The room with its rows of quotations changing second by second, its showers of telegrams, its whirring tickers, stirred Nidstrom's imagination. He was sufficiently new to the environment to dramatize the prosy mechanical fact of its being on an electric circuit with all the big financial battles of the world. The *habitués*, however, seemed to find nothing to admire in that fact. This morning they numbered, perhaps, twenty. Four or five sat in the row of chairs before the largest blackboard studying the quotations from the New York stock market. Others walked about reading the telegrams, watching the tickers, gossiping.

They were absolutely without a distinctive mark. Any twenty men, taken at haphazard from the street, would have done as well. Three of them sat in a sociable group in a corner of the room. The middle of the three, an elderly man of ample frame, with a broad, smooth face made more farmer-like by a pair of gold-bowed spectacles, looked up at Nidstrom as he entered, examined him a moment and went on talking with his companions. Nidstrom turned his back. He knew the big broker; but it was not Maxmann he came to see. Even where he stood the nasal tones of Maxmann's companion on the left penetrated, punctuating the big broker's throaty, mumbling bass. This little man, dapper and quick, dressed with conspicuous disregard for expense, presented so fine a contrast to Maxmann that the two figures would have exactly served a cartoonist as models for his typical confidence man and victim. But Nidstrom knew that if Bannington, who had just promoted a combination of breweries, got any the best of Maxmann he would be entitled to it. The faded and dusty man at Maxmann's right simply listened to the other two. Iron gray muttonchop whiskers curled in toward his rabbit mouth, and he was flabbily fat. Nobody paid any attention to him—one of those vague figures that haunt certain brokers' offices, becoming like a piece of furniture which the *habitués* see without noticing. He appeared every morning when the exchanges opened, nosed purblindly around the tickers and the gossip, made his small plays, and disappeared at two o'clock.

This rear room was connected with the front office of the firm by a narrow passage-way barred by a small solid gate. A youngish man, tall, with a lean face and small features almost like a girl's, came hurrying near-sightedly down this passage-way peering through his glasses. His long, nervous fingers reached for the latch of the gate, but it failed to yield at once and he collided with the obstruction, his thin body half toppling over and his glasses springing from his nose. Half the men in the room laughed.

The junior partner, receiving his glasses from the ready office boy, beamed good-humoredly at the room and gave a high, giggling laugh.

"I usually jump it," he called, in a thin, high voice; "but I didn't get started soon enough this time."

"You did pretty well, though, considering the chance you had," said Nidstrom in an aside, as Gregg came near him, holding a telegram in his hand and peering.

Gregg looked up sharply and sung out in his penetrating voice, "Hullo, Victor. I want to see you a minute. Wait till I find Maxmann."

"Over there," said Nidstrom, indicating the senior partner.

Gregg darted over, bent down and showed the telegram, whispering. In that posture he recognized Maxmann's companions and greeted them as old friends.

The big broker took the telegram, read it deliberately, then slowly crumpled it in his hand and went on talking to the man on his left. Gregg straightened up, but waited. Maxmann tossed the crumpled paper in the direction of a waste-basket and kept on talking; and Gregg slowly withdrew, sidewise, with a kind of frosted expectancy.

When he came back to Nidstrom his failure to make an impression on his father-in-law seemed in no wise to have disconcerted him.

"Was over to see you yesterday," he said. "Arthur told me you'd gone out of town."

"Yes, for the day," said Nidstrom, and then merely by the cumulative weight of his anxiety, he asked, "What's new in Gas?"

Gregg whirled around sharply to face the local blackboard.

"You can see what it's doing," he said;

"eighty-two and three-eighths. Lyman is buying some. It may go up a little, but Lord! it can't hurt you, Victor. You're ten points to the good now." Gregg put his thumbs in the armholes of his red vest and bent confidentially to Nidstrom's ear. "It's going down, I tell you. It's going to the devil. I feel sure of it." He broke into his high laugh and gave Nidstrom's arm a little insinuating shake. "But probably you know more about it than I do. How is the duke nowadays?"

"Oh, just as ever," said Nidstrom, smiling. "I must get to the office."

"Better sell some more," said Gregg, grinning.

"I'll wait awhile," Nidstrom replied.

"Of course you know best. Give me the tip when the time comes," said Gregg.

"No, really, I know nothing," Nidstrom replied gravely; but he saw from the twinkle in Gregg's eye that his friend took the liberty of construing the disclaimer with latitude. As Nidstrom looked at the portentous little ticker he wished for a moment that there were better grounds for Gregg's suspicion.

"Seen *The Eagle* this morning?" Gregg asked. "It says there's going to be an opposition Gas company."

Nidstrom smiled a little. "Leggett is

THE MONEY CAPTAIN

always discovering things in opposition to Mr. Dexter," he suggested.

Gregg leaned over in his nervous, confidential way. "He's dead right this time, Victor," he whispered; "he's even sold some stock. He'll win out, too," the broker added, nodding his head.

Nidstrom smiled more broadly. "I hope so, as long as I'm on that side myself," he said.

He turned to the door with reluctance. That agitated electrical air was his theater just then, and it was like leaving his play in the middle of the performance. It was only by a chance that he found himself involved in this strange and trying affair of the speculation. He had his certain place in the great, intricate machine of Archibald Dexter. His title was assistant secretary of the most important of the several Gas companies through which Dexter constituted himself monopolist and "Duke of Gas," as the newspapers liked to call him. Really his functions were as near as possible to those of private secretary to a man who gave very few confidences and saw to the doing of most things himself. He believed that in that small and remote segment of consciousness where Dexter considered him at all he was the object of a rather friendly interest

THE MONEY CAPTAIN

on the duke's part. There was singularly little of a personal quality in their relations. Nidstrom did his work and the wage was promptly forthcoming; still so far as the personal equation entered at all they met on a level footing. In the bearing of the one man toward the other, their business relations might have been reversed at any instant, making Nidstrom the employer and Dexter the employed, without much change in their manners. Each man in his way had a poise which made a kind of guaranty of respect, and when, ten days before, Dexter gave certain instructions from which Nidstrom perceived that the attorney-general was about to begin a long-threatened attack upon Dexter's combination of companies as being a trust, Nidstrom, after a little reflection, and the business in hand being disposed of, found it perfectly easy to say:

"I have fifty shares of Gas, Mr. Dexter. I shouldn't mind selling it if it is likely to go lower." He gathered up his papers as he spoke, appreciating the value of Dexter's time.

The duke glanced up at him, and became thoughtful for a bare instant. "It's paid for—your Gas?" he asked.

"Oh, yes; I've had it for some time."

"Probably you could buy it back cheaper

later on," said **Dexter** simply. The line of his bearded lips moved very slightly in a smile. "Probably you could buy some more cheaper later on, too," he added, "at least that's my guess." He touched the electric button on his desk, summoning another cog in his wheel, and Nidstrom went out.

Of course it was plainly a hint, a "tip" such as Nidstrom had often thought might one day come to him. Making his little economies and adding the small savings from his wage to the tiny accumulation that grew so slowly, and periodically accusing himself of failing to do the best he could with his money, he had consoled himself with thinking that some day an opportunity would come; then he would be ready for it. In Dexter's office he was in an atmosphere of speculation, yet it had always been something that he had looked at from the outside. Some of the details of those big machinations by which fortunes were seized over night were known to him, but he looked at them a good deal as he looked at the gold plate in the jeweler's show-window. They were for him only in some indefinite and indistinct future. Even after Dexter presented him with the opportunity which he pretended to have been so zealously awaiting, his mind shrank instinctively from the strife and risk of the thing. He tried to tell himself that it was not really the right opportunity at all. Some six months before, after Benjamin Rose, in an accidental moment of his verbal frescoing, had spread before him the dazzling future of Consolidated Gas, he had withdrawn his money from Drouillard's bank and sold his three city bonds and bought fifty shares of Gas. It constituted his capital, and Nell liked to take the newspaper, with proprietary interest, and see what the quotation on Gas was. Now, after he had disciplined himself several times, he took his fifty shares of Gas to Gregg with an order to sell them—and another order to sell two hundred and fifty shares which he did not have but hoped to buy much cheaper later on.

The next day the attorney-general filed his suit in quo-warranto, attacking the charters of the Gas companies, and Gas stock dropped. Nidstrom had many bad moments of misgiving. He hated the effect of cheapness which he saw in himself as, cutting short his lunch, he hurried into an office to look at the ticker and to run eagerly through the telegrams to see what was said of Gas. He found many astonishing things said about it, as the speculation grew. The newspapers took their full share in the proceedings. Those which were unfriendly or

THE MONEY CAPTAIN

hostile to Dexter, which included all excepting the *Clarion*, pointed with an effect of exultation to the decline in Gas shares and drew thence some edifying lessons on the instability of prosperity that was not built on law and equity.

The *Eagle*, which was bitterest of all against Dexter, had a report Monday morning, prominently displayed, that an opposition gas company was forming and would soon apply to the city council for the privilege of laying mains. There was scarcely an hour without some new rumor about Gas, showered down on the brokers' files, ground out of the electric printing machines, and often reflected in the quotations transferred from the whirring, buzzing tickers to the blackboards. Many another amateur besides Nidstrom went with the eddies and falls of the big speculation. Over on Michigan Avenue an ill-clad tailor who made irreproachable clothes for the highest prices rushed to the telephone, nervously pawing his beard, and asked for the quotation on Gas, and felt the pit of his stomach grow cold when the answer came back, "Seventy-nine and a half." On Clark Street an oiled and rosy person, with a flower at his button hole, walked smilingly among the men with bright-hued shirt fronts before his bar,

THE MONEY CAPTAIN

whereon he often bent his elbow, and now and then whispered confidentially to a friend that he was makin' a killin' in Gas.

As the speculation increased its infection spread to new places. Gas shares were falling. It was as though a great stream of money were flowing invisibly down the street and men scented it with a prickling of the nerves as hounds scent blood. Everywhere there was a leaning and listening for news, even by those *habitués* who preserved their air of indifference. When Maxfield, of the *Evening Call*, asked Dolliver what he thought of Gas, that stubby bank president chuckled into his limp shirt front and said that electric lights were good enough for him. From the door of the president's office the great parallelogram of the banking room was visible, with its stretch of counter and long line of tellers' wickets, each having a cluster of electric lights over it, like a miniature street in a roofed city. Men were coming and going across the tiled floor. Behind the long counters and the cages of the tellers, book-keepers toiled at row after row of long desks. Greenbacks and gold were heaped and tossed about here, and carted in and out of the vaults on heavy iron trucks like baser merchandise. There was a high and dull air as of the ultimate temple of money; a

THE MONEY CAPTAIN

high and dull air of exemption from change and chance, as though this were the dead heart of business from whose immutability all the mutable forms of commerce flowed.

Yet when Maxfield went out Dolliver went over to the ticker in the corner and looked at the last quotation on Gas.

A patron said to the assistant cashier, "Gas closes at 79."

The assistant cashier smiled thoughtfully and blinked at his desk. How much he might have made! But caution, bringing virtue with it, returned.

"Dexter'll fool 'em yet," he said oracularly.

That name was everywhere. Dexter was selling. Dexter was buying. Dexter was going to own the new company. Dexter would prevent the new company getting an ordinance. It was Dexter's stock, Dexter's money, Dexter's coup, Dexter's Waterloo.

All the noisy storm revolved around Dexter.

CHAPTER II

In that odd narrow world, walled by the banks and the brokers' offices, which agreed as to nothing except that it was the whole world, there was, however, a diversion to the concentration of attention on Dexter. The newspapers were denounced for that, in attacking Dexter's gas companies, they were the enemies of business; or else for that in controverting attacks on Dexter's gas companies they betrayed their trusts. With readers on both sides of the market the condemnation was unanimous.

Meantime the newspapers breathed scorn for the Stock market and were busy with Dexter on their own account. When the city council, Monday evening, passed an ordinance granting privileges to the Northwestern Gas Company they presented reports the most startling and contradictory. Nobody knew who or what the Northwestern Gas Company was. The alderman who introduced the ordinance confessed that it had been handed to him by a gentleman whose name he had forgotten. Other aldermen, at

THE MONEY CAPTAIN

the naked point of a reportorial interrogation mark, said they voted for the ordinance in deference to an overwhelming public demand for cheaper gas, the new company being restricted to ninety cents a thousand feet, while Dexter charged a dollar. The ordinance had been procured in Dexter's interest, said one; it had been procured in the interest of a powerful party of Boston capitalists who would build competing works and drive Dexter from the field, said another. But whatever else the Northwestern Gas Company and its ordinance were, they were always infamous and reeking with "boodle." The amount paid to the aldermen to pass the ordinance was even named specifically. In fact each paper had a different amount.

And no matter if the ordinance was inimical to Dexter—even as to the same paper the "real facts" in the case often shifted kaleidoscopically from issue to issue—still the harsh wind of editorial criticism blew incessantly about the duke's seasoned ears.

Even the attorney-general was assailed. His motives were impugned either by those who were friendly to Dexter, because he attacked the duke at all; or by the far larger number who were unfriendly to Dexter, because he did not attack more vigorously.

THE MONEY CAPTAIN

The *Eagle* easily led in the hardihood of its assaults, if not in the impression they produced. It demanded of the attorney-general, with innuendo that was obvious, why, if Dexter maintained an illegal combination of gas companies, he was not indicted instead of sued civilly; yet it retorted upon the *Clarion* for insinuating that the state's chief law officer attacked Dexter from personal motives.

"The valued *Clarion*," said an editorial article for the *Eagle* which Leggett was looking over in the proof, "troubles itself about the motives of the attorney-general, or about the motives of anybody who attacks Archibald Dexter. Why should the valued *Clarion* do this? Nobody troubles himself about Mr. Dexter's motive. It is too patent. Everybody knows that he is animated by the single purpose to plunder the public. Why demand that the attorney-general give an exhibition of exalted and impeccable motives? At least while Mr. Dexter's deft hand is engaged in warding off the blows of the state's chief law officer the change in the public's pocket will be comparatively safe. A boy may throw a stone at a dog from mere wantonness; but if the dog is chasing you to bite you, do you reprove the boy?"

THE MONEY CAPTAIN

When Leggett had written O. K. on the margin of the proof, he shouted for the boy who should have been in the outer room. The electric bell was out of order. Most things were out of order in the *Eagle* office. Even the square ancient table at which the editor worked stood insecurely on only three of its fat, carved legs.

Long before, as time is measured in Chicago — that is, fifteen years before — the *Eagle* had been an engine of wealth and power. The special number issued in commemoration of its removal to the new building, three years after the great fire, described the structure as the most magnificent, costly and perfectly equipped newspaper home on earth; a home so large, splendid and well-appointed that any paper besides the *Eagle* would be quite out of place in it. Now, the marble figure of Justice on the top floor, streaked and stained with drippings from the patched, leaky glass dome, looked upon a dismal circle of grimy walls, from which large patches of plaster were missing, disclosing the dirty lath like the ribs of a decaying carcass. Save on the brightest days a naked gas flame burned with a funereal suggestion beside the elevator landing. The figure of Justice was marble, but the pine floor, thrown together in the rush of building, was warped, and the heavy pine doors to the different editorial rooms, once stained to imitate mahogany, had shrunk from the casings and the varnish had peeled and freckled, giving them an unhealthy appearance. Such was the first aspect of the *Eagle*, to a provisional control of which Leggett, then night editor of the *Index*, had been called six months before through an alliance of despairing creditors.

Arthur Franklin had said to Nidstrom, "Leggett in control of the *Eagle* is as interesting as a dynamite bomb in a graveyard."

And it instantly appeared that as to his efficiency there were no cracks or patches or weather stains on the editor. His ruddy cheeks had the smooth hardness of a ripe apple. His lips made a short, straight red line under his close-clipped sandy mustache. There was a hard little dent in his smooth, strong chin where another man might have had a dimple. His sandy hair strung sparsely down on his forehead; and at the center of his scalp a little tuft stood up, humorously. He was made on a large scale and his gray eyes looked out at the world with an effect of being on a rather disrespectfully easy footing with it.

The way he filled his big lungs and shouted for the office boy showed that he had no morbid sensitiveness about being overheard.

The boy for whom he shouted was gone and the tiny ante-room was empty. Thus, Rose, Dexter's chief council, following the direction of the elevator man, came unhindered to the threshold of the editor's room and stood, smiling brilliantly, as Leggett looked up. Coming on this self-appointed mission the lawyer had noted the ill-lighted counting room, the dark passage that led to the creaking elevator, the cracked plastering upstairs; and he was contrasting the august and imperial *Eagle* as it modestly presented itself to its readers on its editorial page with the halt, dismal and bedraggled bird which these forlorn surroundings suggested. There was nothing ill-humored in his appreciation of this contrast—only it was funny—and it argued rather well for him.

"Hello there!" Leggett called, as though it were his long-lost comrade, and he got up holding out his strong hand. When he returned to his chair, the lawyer sat at the end of the ancient table, his dark and powerful eyes shining humorously at the editor. For a moment the two men looked at each other, beaming, and each knowing that the other was taking stock of him. Leggett modestly denied himself the supposition

THE MONEY CAPTAIN

that the busy lawyer, whose time cost clients so dear, had come to see him purely from friendliness. But, whatever Rose had come for, he was ready. The men knew each other well enough, and in a way they liked each other. In the past Leggett had been indebted to Rose for many important views of the inside of affairs, and for his part, he had often willingly worked to the lawyer's ends.

"You're a very approachable editor, anyhow," said Rose. "I didn't know that I should be able to get in."

"Oh, anybody can get in here," Leggett replied, carelessly; "the trouble has been about getting out."

"You don't come to see me any more, now that you've become an editor-in-chief. I didn't know but you'd grown proud."

"Well, I don't have much time for social diversions. Molding public opinion and keeping out of the sheriff's hands at the same time requires pretty close application."

"Doesn't the paper pay?" Rose asked, with a touch of surprise, as though he had supposed it a flourishing institution.

Leggett knew Rose too well to attempt euphuisms. Besides, he did not care. So he answered lightly, "It doesn't pay if it can get the note extended."

THE MONEY CAPTAIN

"Seems to me you're getting out a pretty good paper," said Rose. "I read it every morning."

"Yes, pretty good," said Leggett; "but a newspaper that isn't the best on earth is no good at all. We need better telegraph facilities. I've put my time on the local field so far."

"Yes, you need better telegraph facilities," Rose admitted, "and better mechanical facilities. You ought to have a more presentable office, too." He glanced around him and wondered what else he could suggest that would catch Leggett's fancy. He might mention a beautiful room for the editor-in-chief, with Turkish rugs on the floor and paintings on the wall, like the office of the editor-in-chief of the *Clarion;* but he wasn't sure that Leggett would care for that. "You ought to increase your capital stock," he said.

"Lord, no!" Leggett exclaimed. "Everybody that's had hold of the paper in the last dozen years has increased the capital stock. I forget what it is now, but it's about the same as the First National Bank's. What we want is more money."

"Have you ever seen anybody with a view to getting in some more money?" Rose asked, with a neighborly interest.

THE MONEY CAPTAIN

"Oh, that's in Bascom's hands, I suppose," Leggett answered carelessly, as though he didn't really know.

"Why in Bascom's hands?" the lawyer suggested, still with his air of neighborly interest.

"Well, Bascom represents a majority of the stock, I guess," Leggett replied.

"Bascom—or the people that have lent money," Rose suggested again. He looked over at Leggett an instant and slightly elevated his eyebrows. "Really, I don't see the necessity of waiting for Bascom," he said. "You're doing all the work of building up the paper. If it's to be a success, why not make it your success and get the benefits. Of course all this is gratuitous," he added quickly, with a little wave of his white hand. "Only I'm a friend of the court."

"Of the prisoner," Leggett corrected. "I suppose some money might be got in," he added indefinitely—"and it could be used to advantage."

"Undoubtedly," said the lawyer.

Each of the men felt that the conversation had come to an issue, and the lawyer felt that the issue was in his hands. Sitting at the end of that ancient table under the cracked plastering, smiling through his carefully trimmed brownish beard in which there was not a line of gray, with his air of amiable neighborly interest slightly touched with humor, and bearing his easy effect of full-blown prestige and success, Rose's wit played upon the situation as a cat holds a playful but alert paw over a mouse. And for once, with all his subtlety, he went wrong.

The two men knew each other well enough, but it went without saying that Rose knew Leggett in a suppler consciousness. In the lawyer's deft and busy brain all things bore their relation near or remote to the big plans that were constantly weaving through his fingers. Dexter as much as anybody else he regarded from an under side. He liked Leggett very well and he knew a force in him, but not the real force. He knew Leggett's impudence, but missed his pride. He thought him an ambitious, hardy young man who was trying to attract attention by the mere volume of noise he could make. He did not know that in certain exigencies Leggett would be wholly capable of Samson's stroke. He did not know that in getting control of the *Eagle* Leggett came into the opportunity for power as a man finally coming into his own. It did not occur to him that the hardy, humorous young man opposite, with the mop of sandy hair over his square forehead, now regarded him as from

THE MONEY CAPTAIN

a level footing; from a standpoint far different from that of his reporting days when he had been willing enough to do little journalistic chores for the influential lawyer in return for a piece of news.

Looking over at Rose, amiably also, a certain prospect unrolled before Leggett, and he examined it for an instant—to become Dexter's pensioner, if he failed to become his conqueror; to conduct an organ in Dexter's interest, if he failed to make the *Eagle* an instrument for his overthrow. A word, he thought, would put him in the way of accomplishing the alternate possibility. Dexter's figure, as he constructed it in his imagination, came before him, slightly smiling, slightly supercilious and scornful as having paid the price and acquired a cheap accession, namely, himself and his *Eagle*. He waited, quite willing that Rose should say more, as the man with a trustworthy weapon waits to surprise his assailant.

But Rose was not minded to go further. He wished the next word to come from Leggett. A moment elapsed; then Leggett observed casually, "How's the law business?"

Rose brushed it aside with a quick, "Oh, I'm always busy." He glanced at the clock on the wall. "I'm waited for now."

THE MONEY CAPTAIN

Leggett smiled. "Very good of you to run up," he said. "I should come around to see you if I could ever get away."

Rose got up. If he felt piqued he did not show it. "It might be worth your while," he said, good-humoredly. "I suppose I might give up some news now and then if the editor-in-chief came around for it."

Leggett's newspaper sense aroused. "Anything new?" he asked.

Rose considered a moment. "Nothing now," he replied; "but there's likely to be almost any time." Standing at the end of the table quite at his ease, he said, without the batting of an eyelid, "I'm glad to see you treating this gas matter decently."

Leggett, also quite unabashed, murmured, "Oh, we treat everything decently, you know."

With the effect of a more personal address, Rose said, "I should like to see you succeed here, Leggett; I believe you will. If I can be of any service, you know—"

"Yes," said Leggett; "very good of you. I shan't forget." In a way it was a sincere word on both sides, and the men shook hands and parted in a tiny glow of regard. As Rose went away he thought, "Leggett is a good fellow after all; he'll come around in a few days." Leggett thought, "Good old Rose—I almost wish that I were of a sort to sell out to him."

When the lawyer had disappeared the editor took up the proof he had laid on the desk and re-read it. The allusion to the dog struck him as beautifully insulting, and he marked the article for double leads. Its appearance in the *Eagle* next day would, of course, be a renewed and more irretrievable declaration of war. Well, the faster and hotter it came the better it would suit him. It was not so much that he hated Dexter as that he despised him. To him Dexter was not first of all a public enemy. That was rather incidental. The conception of Dexter on which his antagonism was primarily based was that of a cheap and vulgar upstart; a fellow from the kitchen pompously obtruding himself in the parlor. He, Hamilton Leggett, wished to kick this scullion duke, to measure strength with him, to feel him give way in his hands. He had no equivocations for himself. Independence and power was the goal. The man who put his foot on Dexter's thick neck would be a person to be reckoned with. And with all this there were two remarkable, lustrous brown eyes, a prettily modeled chin, a roll of lightish bronze hair over two pink ears—he wished to take her the fragments of the duke in his coat pocket and to roll them out in her lap and say, "See what expensive bric-a-brac I've brought you."

CHAPTER III

For a moment, as Rose went down the worn stone steps that led from the counting room of the *Eagle* to the flagging, after an obsolete architectural fashion, he indulged in a glimpse of himself benignly handing Leggett up from his financial slough of misguided opposition to a comfortable seat in the ducal establishment. He did not doubt that he was going to do Leggett a kindness— his own intervention in fact was simply that injection of perspicacious good sense which so often was all that was needed to put a bad situation quite right.

He had known Leggett for four or five years, and had always known him to be tractable and serviceable enough in a careless kind of way. He thought pleasantly of the strong, ruddy-faced young man whose effect was at once that of being on easy, chummy terms with the world.

However, other things came to the lawyer's mind as he walked briskly along Washington Street, his athletic and well-kept figure moving with an effect of ease and assurance. It was Dexter himself who waited.

The Gas Building stood on Dearborn Street, its six stories of dingy brick confessing an ancient epoch as compared with the skyscrapers that towered leanly in the neighborhood. On one side of the marble rotunda a pair of iron stairs clinging to the curving wall led up to the public office of the principal Gas Company—a bank-like room, with rows of book-keepers' desks behind the windowed counter. On the other side a similar stair led to the banking house of Drouillard & Co. Dexter's and the other managerial offices were on the top floor. It was part of the lawyer's magnificence that he kept a perfect effect of independence in this country of the duke's, which was a little state in itself, having its own cabals and jealousies, like a court, but presenting a solid front against the common enemy, whoever or whatever the enemy might be.

Entering the square and bare ante-room on the top floor, Rose nodded good-naturedly to the tall office boy and glanced at his watch. The boy hastily wrote the lawyer's name on a slip of paper and carried it inside, exactly as though Rose had been any other caller.

Four or five men sat around the ante-room waiting for an audience. There were several

THE MONEY CAPTAIN

vacant chairs; but Rose remained standing. Nidstrom came out of the inner room, his hands full of papers. He nodded familiarly to the lawyer, and Rose, as by inadvertence, crossed the secretary's path, made a slight elevation of his dark eyebrows and gave his head a little jerk, questioningly, toward the inner room.

"A reporter just went in," said Nidstrom, in a low voice, smiling a little.

Rose smiled also, as though satisfied, and a moment later the office boy appeared, holding open the inner door, his head drooped forward, looking at Rose as inviting him to enter.

The lawyer went through the open door briskly and the door closed behind him. One of the waiting men sighed resignedly and lit a cigar. The others shifted to easier positions in their chairs. All of them knew the trig, assured figure, with the dark beard trimmed in Parisian style. The one with the cigar, sliding down in his chair, growled over his coat collar, "That means another half-hour anyway—lucky if it ain't an hour." His neighbor gave his chair a hitch and swore impatiently. Then they settled down to waiting and began discussing in low tones the project which was so important to them that they were willing to spend half an after-

THE MONEY CAPTAIN

noon in Dexter's ante-room for the chance of getting from him the three words that were necessary to set it going.

Behind the closed door, Rose nodded to Dexter, crossed leisurely and sat down in the leather chair midway of the long table in the center of the room. The man from the *Clarion* sat in the chair at the end of Dexter's desk, leaning forward and talking. Dexter was calmly signing a pile of type-written letters, listening to the reporter without looking up; but his composed face expressed the utmost good-nature.

The room was first of all a work-shop. A colored chart under the plate-glass top of the long table showed the mains of Dexter's six Gas Companies, reaching to every part of the city, and there were some mechanical models on the desk at which Dexter sat. His coarse and stiff beard, bluish black in color and trimmed close to his round face, showed only here and there a white thread. His black hair bristled up stubbornly over his broad, low forehead. The thick, close-cut beard left a little ruddy disk of each cheek; yet his aspect was not that of a young man, and the reporter knew that he was nearly fifty. He was short and thick as to his body. He sat sidewise to the desk, bending forward slightly to sign the pile

THE MONEY CAPTAIN

of type-written letters before him, his gray felt hat on the back of his head, where it seemed to be caught in the bristles of his hair. The attitude thrust his paunch into prominence and made him look stouter than he appeared when standing. This figure, about which all the breathless strivings of the street then centered, gave at once the effect of a perfect poise, a complete self-possession. When he glanced up at the reporter and nodded, his eye twinkling good-naturedly, the line of his mouth moving in a slight smile as though some joke were afoot, and said, calmly, "Well, what worries you to-day?" that atmosphere of nervous striving, of frenzying uncertainty, of rumors and hazards out of which the man had just come, seemed at once to fall away and become remote and cheap.

Dexter went on signing the letters as the man talked. He glanced up now and then with that movement of the lips which was only the beginning of a smile when the man apologetically brought forward a particularly improbable report. By the time the man finished his brief review of the situation in the street the letters were signed. Dexter shoved them to a corner of the desk and touched a bell button. He spoke very calmly, with his air of perfect poise, as from

THE MONEY CAPTAIN

a high, serene center of assurance. He knew nothing of any opposition gas company, except what he had seen in the newspapers.

"I'm not bothering about it," he said. "If anybody wants to start another gas company the field is open. I suppose they'll start their company and lay a few miles of mains and fail to make expenses and come around and beg me to buy 'em out, and if I do it the newspapers will make a terrible hullabaloo and say I'm bound to be a monopolist. Well, I'm not bound to be a monopolist at all. If there's nobody else in the gas business it's just because I make and sell gas cheaper than anybody else can. As to the attorney-general's suit, we will fight that out in court. I've noticed that Gas stock is lower, but I don't care anything about that. I'm not selling or buying any. The only thing I look at is the earnings of the companies and they are satisfactory to me. Probably somebody got scared and threw over some stock—and of course that's exactly what the gentlemen who engineered the break in the market were after."

He nodded the reporter out with a good-natured air of having solved all his doubts; and as the reporter slipped through the door the duke turned calmly to Rose. Probably

THE MONEY CAPTAIN

it did not occur to him that Rose must know he had been lying to the reporter. He had been performing one of the small, necessary functions of his office—serenely, unfalteringly, with precision, as he performed all other functions of his office. He turned to the lawyer with an untroubled face and a mind single to the work before them.

Rose came over to the vacated chair and they began discussing certain aspects of the attorney-general's suit.

Only certain aspects of things were to be discussed with Rose. The lawyer held his white hands conspicuously in front of him. If questionable things were to be done he went into a godlike trance until they were accomplished. He looked out for his own conscience, and he presumed politely that other people looked out for theirs. There may have been a place—in one of the sub-cellars of his consciousness—where Rose judged Dexter. But that judgment had nothing to do with their intercourse, which was on the pure, single footing of business. Their rise had been contemporaneous. Twenty years before, in Dexter's first venture—with a small, precarious suburban gas company—Rose was junior member of the law firm that had been consulted. And all the big maneuvers that had followed had received the benefit of the lawyer's ingenious mind. It had been not merely a campaign, but a continuous pitched battle. Not at one juncture only, but at several, Rose had seen Dexter put his whole fortune at hazard and await the issue with perfectly steady eyes. That appealed to Rose's admiration. Many times the lawyer, with his amiable air, had discovered broad practicable passes through mountainous opposition. Dexter had a very solid, commercial appreciation of the value of that ingenious gift. Personally the two men scarcely chimed. Each was a very positive quality. And their tastes were different. For example, Rose would not have lied to the reporter, and he would not have worn the rather shabby trousers which the duke found entirely adequate. At times when something was to be carried through the city council Rose turned his back; just as when Dexter thought it advisable to copiously damn a caller, the lawyer looked thoughtfully at the ceiling.

"What do you think of Deere?" Dexter asked presently.

Rose fingered his beard leisurely. "He impresses me as a bright young man," he said, as contemplating an interesting little object from his serene height.

Dexter tapped with the ends of his fingers

THE MONEY CAPTAIN

on the desk, thoughtfully. "I don't know," he said with a faint note of discontent. "He's pretty slim. He looks pretty nervous. I don't like men whose nerves might get flighty." He brushed his hand across his brow and his fingers dropped to his upper vest pocket. "Well," he said, decisively, "he seems to be more available than anybody else."

Rose waited, offering no suggestion.

Dexter drew out a cigar and bit off the end.

"I thought that was forbidden," said Rose, good-humoredly.

"Yes," said Dexter, a little dully. "Oh, damn it!" he added with impatience, "I can't be bothering all the time about those things. I've got to keep this business going—and I couldn't if I spent all my time following doctors' rules."

Presently, of the attorney-general, Rose observed, "He has the newspapers to reckon with."

"Oh, the newspapers! They'll pitch into him whatever he does." Dexter spoke with contempt. "I see the *Eagle* is going for him now because he doesn't have me indicted."

"Leggett is pretty bitter," the counsel suggested.

THE MONEY CAPTAIN

"He's a rather irritating blackguard," Dexter confessed calmly; "but I don't mind him."

"I dropped in to see him this afternoon," said the lawyer casually.

"What for?" Dexter asked, abruptly.

"It was my own notion," Rose replied. "I'd like to get him in a more satisfactory position—his paper, I mean."

"I don't know's it's worth bothering about," said Dexter carelessly. "You'll always have some of those flies buzzing around you. My idea is to let 'em buzz and be damned. They can't do anything but make a noise."

"I think you're wrong," said Rose, with perfect assurance. "It's bad playing to overlook any points. Best have even the flies on your side."

Dexter looked up with a bending of the line of his bearded lips, his eyes twinkling. "You're more than half a Jew," he said.

Rose got up. "Well, a small thing—a fly or a cigar—may do large harm."

"You have to take your chances," Dexter replied a little absently, as he rung for the office boy and looked at the cards to see who should come in next.

The interview with Dexter in the *Clarion*

THE MONEY CAPTAIN

next morning was introduced with an effect of setting at rest all doubts about Gas stock, and the paper said that it would doubtless steady the market. Yet Nidstrom, whose personal interest was not to have the market steadied, felt no disquietude on account of the interview. He had seen a good many others, and he only smiled a little in a half mournful way. He wished that Dexter wouldn't do these things. But of course his wish didn't count.

The interview was smiled over in some other places; notably behind the closed doors of Drouillard's private room in the banking office of Drouillard & Co. on the ground floor. Drouillard sat on one side of the small table and Gregg faced him; the paper, opened to the interview, lying between them. The banker was very stout. He had a big, fat face that managed to be handsome in spite of his puffiness. He was very stylishly dressed and he wore always an effect of being shiny and bulging with prosperity. He leaned back in his chair, his thick legs thrust under the table, wide apart. Gregg bent over the table, his eyes twinkling eagerly at Drouillard through his glasses.

"Ain't he a bird!" said the broker in tones of exultation.

"Yes, when it comes to lying," said the

banker. "Why, I know positively of a thousand shares that came from up-stairs."

"Of course," Gregg piped back excitedly. "I tell you, Jack, Dexter is unloading that Gas stock and it's going to the devil, sure."

Ten minutes later, when the broker emerged from the room, his face was decorously composed; but he was bubbling within. His nervous fingers, slender and fragile-looking, clutched at freedom, at security, at relief from Maxmann's stolid tyranny. In marrying Maxmann's daughter he had wedded a tenuous place in the big firm; but it was not a blessed portion. Maxmann snubbed him as openly in the office as Mrs. Gregg did at home. Worse than all, Maxmann treated his opinions with massive contempt—that big, ignorant, stupid Maxmann who really had but a thimbleful of logy brains.

When Gregg entered the customers' room at his own office he even tried a joke with his father-in-law, and he beamed on everybody else. But, as the clock hands moved slowly toward the hour for the opening of the stock exchange, a belated trouble beset him and grew acute. Presently he gathered his courage and sidled up to Maxmann.

"Drouillard is selling some Gas," he whispered.

THE MONEY CAPTAIN

Maxmann turned his grave, farmer-like gaze upon the junior member an instant, then nodded his head, and Gregg felt relieved.

CHAPTER IV

Leaning against an iron pillar under the huge arched iron and glass roof of the train shed, Nidstrom waited. To the left the dim waters of the lake moved with soft restlessness in the twilight under the droaning patter of a gentle rain. Off to the north the lighthouse on the end of the pier took deliberate alternating red and white glances at him. A solitary man paced nervously up and down the platform, also waiting, and three women in a subdued group wondered if the train would be late. To the south, amid a dimly grotesque tangle of colored switch lights and cars and smoky dark, a locomotive headlight suddenly appeared, glaring at the station. It darted first to right, then to left, then disappeared abruptly as a Cyclopean eye might wink shut. Nidstrom went back to his pillar, patiently resigned to delay, the women exclaimed aggrievedly, and the solitary man took to his pacings. A moment later another headlight appeared. The men in blouses began pushing their trucks close to the track. A couple of red-capped attendants

THE MONEY CAPTAIN

came from behind the roofed entrance to a subway and started down the platform. Nidstrom was conscious of a slight aching sensation behind his knees, as though he had walked far. The locomotive swept by him at diminishing speed, straining and quivering with power, drawing its long line of black coaches. An instant later passengers began debarking endlessly; and Nidstrom watched the stream of faces with quickening heart. Hundreds went by, it seemed to him; and then he saw Nell's face looking toward him, a little way down, and it seemed that her appearance had followed instantly upon the stopping of the train. She stopped as he hurried toward her, and he heard a sweet treble saying, "But I don't see papa!" A little figure, topped with a red cap, with yellow, flying hair, came running toward him, with arms outstretched.

As they came to the entrance of the station, Nell, as though it were a matter of course, started across to the tiny waiting-room where they could take the suburban train. But Nidstrom called, "This way!" and in an instant he was putting Tots through the open door of a hack, then bundling Nell in and climbing in himself, cumbered with bags, and the door was shut on them before Nell had time to protest.

THE MONEY CAPTAIN

"Why, Victor," she began reprovingly, "you ought not to do this. We can just as well go home by the train."

And Tots, slowly adjusting a delighted mind to the prospect, put in an excited pipe: "Are—are—we going to wide home in this?"

The man put out his arms and gathered the child into his exultant laughter. "Certainly," he said; "we're nobs now."

"You ought to be scolded," said Nell. She used much the same authoritative air with him that she did with the baby. "We can't afford a carriage." In the dim light her smooth cheek shone like marble and her dark eyes were luminous.

"It's my treat," said Nidstrom. "You don't come home every day." The beaming with which he regarded his wife broadened his face, which was too broad at its best.

"I decided that you were worth a dollar and a half extra to-day. Besides, I know what you've been used to the last month up there at High Grove among all your old beaux, and I don't want the contrast to be too painful."

It was too dark to see; but he imagined her glance, and he chuckled at it. He would have chuckled at the rain if there had been nothing else. He felt the atmosphere of her

THE MONEY CAPTAIN

presence with a lonely man's precious sense of snuggling down into his own comfortable little world again.

He had once put it before himself as an incontrovertible proposition that an unpliable fellow, well on toward thirty, with no money to speak of and only his clerk's wage, had no right to think of marrying a girl like Nell Franklin. When the failure of Franklin's corporate employer brought the family's fortunes to a dead wall the marriage came about quite inevitably, as though it had been the sign they found on the wall. The ceremony was performed in the parlor of the house on Tremont Avenue—under a floral bell so big that it put the rest of the room vastly out of proportion. At once he had taken to his home with an effect of having been long exiled from it.

When Nell was away visiting her father and mother at the country town to which they had returned after two decades' failure in the city, forlornness devoured him. Of evenings he sat on the front step smoking his cigar with a kind of uncouth and pathetic helplessness to find any really friendly spot in the world. Or, he strolled aimlessly around the streets of the neighborhood paying a new home-sick pang to every snug family group clustered on its steps or get-

THE MONEY CAPTAIN

ting the most out of its little grass-plot. Melancholy fancies assailed him.

Going home after dark in the suburban train, the endless processions of the fronts of houses and of the backs of flats, each twinkling with its little lights, by which the car sped, impressed him as mournfully fragile little shelters, holding together from day to day, but momentarily liable to ruin from any small, commonplace mischance to the man who brought in the money. In the long, swiftly unfolding panorama there were hints of grandeur, as, at Sixteenth Street and further down, in opening spaces the shapes of great houses appeared, solid, costly, imposing, and the façades of vast hotels, innumerably jeweled with electric lights, where all the details of luxurious living were ready to one's hand at the touch of a bell. Yet, as he thought, few of these imposing places were secure. In most of them the cost and the chances were anxiously reckoned, and it was as though the real landlord, an intangible being, stood over all of them impassively ready to turn out one tenant and take in the next. Elsewhere, along miles of galleries protruding from the backs of flat buildings the homely operations of the household were exposed to view. One could look into a kitchen and see people eating; or, the

THE MONEY CAPTAIN

family sat in the gallery for the sight and coolness of the lake, the man in his shirt-sleeves, the woman going and coming, all with a curious effect to Nidstrom's imagination as of being abruptly projected into sight for a moment; the next to sink back in oblivion. At moments it would appear to him that the whole huge city was but an uneasy camp whose innumerable phantom officers were continually whispering to stricken ears the command: "Step down. Move out." Ah, it might be coming to him to-morrow! He would then need a new grip of his doggedness in respect of the Gas speculation. Even familiar little Tremont Avenue would turn an unfriendly face to him. The houses of the block in which he lived were just alike on both sides of the street—plain two-story affairs trimmed with brick. From this similarity of design the knowing recognized them at once as having been built in a lot to sell on the installment plan. This sameness gave the street a certain toy-like effect which Arthur Franklin, his brother-in-law, liked to make fun of.

This evening of Nell's return the recollection of his alienation heightened his satisfaction, just as the storm, looked at through a snug window, is pleasant to the man who has escaped from it.

THE MONEY CAPTAIN

Nell leaned back in the shabby but comfortable seat. "Well, it is pleasanter than waiting for the train and walking in the rain," she admitted, smiling a little at his delight. She was slender and she wore dresses with an effect of drapery, which, perhaps, distinguished her a little among women in shirt waists. It was her eyes and her voice that came to Nidstrom most frequently in the lonely hours when he missed her—eyes very dark, very gentle and unflinching, and a serene voice.

The child stood up on the front seat, clinging to the padded back of it and peering intently through the window at the lighted, rainy boulevard. Attracted by the child, the man and woman leaned forward now and then to look from the snugness of the shabby hack. At one house in particular—the largest and costliest on the boulevard—they both looked long and silently. An electric lantern burned in the recess of its granite, fortress-like porch as though to light the owner to a mediæval security against the chances of this rainy world. Dexter lived there.

"I should think he would be lonesome," Nell suggested.

Nidstrom thought of it a moment. "No, I don't believe he is. He's always busy, you

THE MONEY CAPTAIN

know, and that seems to be all he wants. After all, he's got to be a sort of machine. He has his niece and, sometimes, his wife."

"But it isn't a real home," Nell persisted; "just that invalid wife and a young lady niece; no children."

"We might take the poor man in! We might surround the unfortunate creature with the comforts of a real home!" Nidstrom laughed.

When the hack drew up in Tremont Avenue, Martha came down the steps in the light rain, in honest, hen-like agitation, and it took her a moment to comprehend clearly that they had come home in a carriage without anybody being disabled.

Nidstrom, carrying the muffled child, followed Nell into the hall, and instantly the house, which had seemed forlorn and empty while she and Victor were away, brimmed with cheer; its atmosphere, in which he had detected a funereal suggestion, became cozy and charming the moment her voice sounded within the door. There was only the front room and a dining-room and kitchen on one side the hall, and on the other side a place they called the library because Nidstrom sat in there to smoke. Nearly all of the furnishings had been taken over, with the house itself, from the Franklins. Mrs. Franklin's tastes were rather violent; but the things were comfortable enough, and Nell and Nidstrom agreed that, for the present, while the house was being paid for, that was the important point. Martha also was part of the Franklin *régime*—the most valued of the lot. When there was company she kindly played the part of servant to her wards.

Now, Nell followed her into the dining-room and kitchen without removing her hat, and for a long time, as it seemed to Nidstrom, he heard their voices in the kitchen going over some household economics while the child cuddled and drowsed in his arms and he kept going over possible methods of presenting the grand surprise. He followed Nell up-stairs when she took Victor to bed, and waited for her in the front room where they commonly sat together. Nidstrom, sitting by the window, looking down into the rainy street, could hear Nell's voice humming a lullaby. Presently she came slipping through the curtains and drew a chair near his, smiling, as though finally accepting herself as being definitely at home. "Well," she said, "what have you been doing this week? Your letters haven't been very satisfactory."

Nidstrom's hand went to his inside pocket and he drew out a folded slip of shiny brown

THE MONEY CAPTAIN

paper—he had felt of it a dozen times since dinner.

"There's the most I've been doing," he said, handing her the paper, with a smile that was half apologetical. For, after all, it seemed rather commonplace, not at all with the dramatic quality he had imagined.

Nell took the paper, smiling a little and half suspecting a joke. She unfolded it; glanced down at it; then looked quickly up at her husband, a little startled and much puzzled. She saw Nidstrom's name, after the printed words, "Pay to the Order of," then "Twelve Thousand" and the name of a bank and some further words and figures. Nidstrom met her look with a broadening of his apologetical smile. She examined the paper again.

"What is it, dear?" she asked gravely. She knew that it was money, that it purported to be their money, and she felt bewildered.

"Money," said Nidstrom; "our money. We're as rich as Dexter, lacking a few millions."

"Is it—really—yours?" she asked, doubtfully.

"Yours and mine and Tots's," Nidstrom answered.

"But where did you get it?" Nell asked

gravely. With a growing weight of anxiety, she added, pleadingly, "Tell me all about it at once." The illegible scrawl at the bottom of the check gave her no clew; but she saw the card of the firm printed across the top. "Maxmann & Gregg—is that the Mr. Gregg I know, and his father-in-law?"

"Yes," said Nidstrom, "they're stock brokers." He pulled himself together, reluctantly, to tell her about it.

"Well," he began, "you see, I sold our fifty shares of Gas stock, and with that money for margin I sold a lot more that I didn't own. The stock went down. This is the profit. I bought back our fifty shares, so that stands just as it did before. Everything is just the same except we're this much ahead."

"I shouldn't think Mr. Dexter would like you to do that," she commented quickly, her unformulated antagonism to this new thing striking at the first point which presented itself.

"Why, it was Dexter who put me in the way of it—he gave me a 'tip' as they say. Anyhow I took what he said to mean that, and I tried it—and won; you know, first the attorney-general brought a suit against the companies and that affected the stock and then, last Monday. the City Council passed an ordinance granting privileges to a new company—the Northwestern Gas Company. It's supposed to be in opposition to Mr. Dexter's companies, and it's going to sell gas for ninety cents and the stock went still lower."

"Isn't that the ordinance the newspapers are saying so much about—saying it was got through by bribery?" Nell asked, with a new touch of apprehension. Her mind was still groping around the puzzle.

"Yes, that's the one," said Nidstrom; "but the newspapers are always crying 'boodle.' They don't know any more about this ordinance than they have known about a dozen others that they said the same things about. You see, I took the chance and won. The money is good. Think what it means to you and me and Tots. If it doesn't make us independent it helps us toward independence. It goes a good ways toward taking us out of that hand-to-mouth uncertainty that no mere hired man, nor his family, can be free from."

"Oh, I know that, dear," Nell replied quickly. "I'm as glad of the money as you are. It's —splendid—only, well, it took me by surprise, you see, and—and—"

She looked over at her husband, not knowing just how to say the thing in her mind. The actual processes of the money-getting

THE MONEY CAPTAIN

were hopelessly beyond her; but in the lump she recognized a stock-exchange transaction, a speculation. She knew that men did those things, that in the large, obscure world of business they had their place. She knew that out of their esoteric processes came definite results—namely, fortune and ruin. She had always had her silent pride in managing the money-affairs of the family. It was her little economical contrivings—and they were something very precious to her—which enabled them to add to their savings. There was a kind of tacit agreement that Nidstrom was impracticable. Yet he had made this tremendous stroke without letting her know anything about it.

"I shouldn't like you to do this, dear," she said ineffectually. She could scarcely have said just where it wounded her.

"Well, I'm not going to hang out a shingle, if that's what you mean," Nidstrom replied. Secretly he felt a little rebuffed and unfairly used. He disliked the atmosphere of the speculation as much as she did. Still, he had won, and he would have liked her to pamper, at least a little, his man's sense of having triumphed, of having come out of the struggle with his laurels while so many others were struggling empty-handed; and he would have liked her to appreciate more keenly the

THE MONEY CAPTAIN

difference that the money made—a little citadel and rock for both of them.

"I should always have blamed myself if I hadn't taken this opportunity," he said. "A man with a wife and child has no right to overlook a chance to make money that comes in his way—if he hasn't any to speak of. He hasn't even a right to be too nice in his scruples as to how he makes it. Of course he can draw the line somewhere; but he mustn't coddle his sensitiveness, if he has any. It's exactly like getting bread for them. If he minds a little mud he simply acts selfishly and fails in his duty to them. If I should die it would be infinitely worse for me to leave you and Tots unprovided for—to plunge you down into the struggle of bread-getting—than that I should trample on some of my pretty delicacies—supposing me to have any—in making a decent provision for you. And this was right enough, too; Mr. Dexter put me in the way of it."

"Oh, yes, it was right enough," Nell answered, rather absently; "and the money is good to have." Suddenly her mind caught at something and she looked up with a new interest. "But if these things—this attack by the attorney-general and this new ordinance—were in opposition to Mr. Dexter, how did he know about them to tell you?"

"I don't know that he did know," said Nidstrom; "although," he added truthfully, "I guess he did. As to how he knew—well, for me it's sort of looking a gift horse in the mouth, you know; and, anyway, I'm not bound to inquire. I simply take the money and am mighty thankful to get it."

Nell leaned back in her chair and looked down at the shiny strip of paper. Presently, as though a fascination came out of it, she began to smile. "It is good," she admitted. "Now I know that Victor can have his education. Why, with this twelve thousand dollars and the house all paid for and the Gas stock we're almost rich!" suddenly she laughed. "I shan't be deferential to Mrs. Thompson any more when she mentions her coachman and three maids."

"No," said Nidstrom, "you needn't be. You can say that I'm thinking of setting up a carriage. We could have a sort of one-horse carriage if we liked. You see this will bring in six hundred a year, fifty dollars a month—and we can just lavish that on all sorts of luxuries."

Nell's dark eyes laughed back at him; her fine even teeth shone through her parted lips. "You can lavish one month, and I'll lavish the next," she said. "We'll take turns being swells· and outside the house the poor one mustn't even speak to the one who's lavishing. My month I'll hire a carriage and drive by the Gas office at lunch time and look at you through a thing with a handle."

"Maybe I'd look first-rate through something with a handle," said Nidstrom. "I don't believe anybody ever tried me that way. I guess my first luxury will be to prosecute the Illinois Central under the smoke ordinance. I'd rather do that than own a yacht."

"But that would take too long," Nell objected. "If it hadn't been settled by the last day of your month you'd have to sneak away like Cinderella when her coach turned back to a pumpkin."

"Well, I'd say to the lawyers, 'I have no more money to carry on this suit, but there's a very wealthy lady living with me; maybe she'll lend me some.'"

"The wealthy lady wouldn't, though," Nell declared with triumph. "If she began that her swellness would go away and never come back. And do you know," she added abruptly, sparkling, "I was half afraid of this at first, really!"

She thought that over for a moment, and became quite sober. "Honestly, at first, it seemed a kind of calamity," she confessed, smiling gravely. "After all, dear, we've

THE MONEY CAPTAIN

been very happy—and Tots has grown so splendidly. It seemed somehow like a change."

Nidstrom, too, became thoughtful. It brought up the ultimate aspect of the new money—the one perhaps that he cared most about and which he was most doubtful about.

In a moment he looked over at her in a troubled way.

"Well," he admitted, "it did suggest a change to me."

"A change! How?" Nell asked quickly.

"Why, I don't know very definitely," he replied—"but something in the country; something of our very own, you know."

"To move to the country, do you mean? To live there?" Nell asked, astonished.

For a moment Nidstrom did not reply. He sat with his big head drooping forward, thinking. It was not quite easy to make her see the thing that was so absolutely convincing to him. He said, abruptly, "Oh, you know there's a bad air around here, a detestable air; everything here is more or less given over to this grasping and contriving. A man must give up his life to business drudgery. Abroad if a man makes money he goes to the country, where he can have some repose, some margin to his life. These cities are detestable. Of course I haven't

THE MONEY CAPTAIN

thought very much about it," he added hastily.

"You wouldn't like the country, dear," said Nell, quietly, sympathetically; and the man felt in her manner of saying it, in the look from her soft black eyes, that quality of opposition, uncontentious but unyielding, which he knew in her. He felt, too, as he had so many times before, that in some way he stood accused of being rather impracticable, rather whimsical and fanciful.

"Well, we'll see later on," he said, smiling.

"But what are you going to do with the money now?" Nell asked. It had all come back to matter of fact.

"I've scarcely made up my mind," Nidstrom replied slowly. "Of course, I can buy some bonds." He was silent a moment and reached over and took the check from his wife's hands. "I don't know but I closed the deal too soon," he said, looking at the check and not at his wife. "Gas stock is lower now and Gregg thinks it's bound to be still lower. Mr. Dexter might possibly say something further about the stock. If we had about twice as much we could really go into the country if we wished."

"But you wouldn't go into that again!" Nell exclaimed, with so genuine a touch of

THE MONEY CAPTAIN

alarm that Nidstrom laughed helplessly. It hurt him too a little. He wished again that she would realize the fact that he had made a lot of money when so many other men who were not accused of being impracticable were trying to make money and failing. He thought, in the light of the check, that he ought to have something taken off from the handicap of impracticableness which he felt that his wife invented for him.

"Oh, I'm not going into anything right now," he said. "I'll deposit the money with Drouillard for the present."

"It will be safe there, won't it?" Nell asked, to reassure herself.

Nidstrom laughed. "I might let you and Martha hide it for me," he said. "Or, I might ask Drouillard to give a bond."

He folded the check with an air of carelessness and tucked it in his vest pocket; and the anxious air with which Nell followed the bit of paper amused him mightily. When she looked down at the pocket after he had removed his hand he laughed at her as though she had fallen into his trap.

"That's the trouble with getting rich," he said; "it brings out the latent miserliness of people."

He said it quite good-humoredly. At the same time he wished that she had not looked so grave when he spoke of the country. He thought that possibly he had earned his dream. He did not accuse her of putting her opinion above his selfishly. But he could have wished that the inevitable difference between two minds had worked out along another line and left him freer in this one respect. However, the difference was part of the condition, and it was in recognition of her essential unselfishness that he got up and put his arm over her shoulder.

"We'll try to do the best with the money," he said; "especially for Totterolorum's sake. It's more for him than for either of us, anyhow. He must have a swell month if we miss ours altogether."

By a common impulse they moved over to the alcove. Nell pulled the curtain aside a little and they peered down at the sleeping child exultantly.

CHAPTER V

The money made almost no difference in the Nidstroms' way of living. Victor bought two boxes of a more expensive brand of cigars and smoked them with an uneasy conscience while he tried to bully Nell into a justifying extravagance. She took the money with which he expected her to hire a cab for her one social diversion—a bi-weekly whist club—and bought young Victor's fall underwear at a bargain ahead of its season. Then Nidstrom put the cigars aside for company and fell back on a briar pipe.

Even when they decided to give a little dinner as a surreptitious celebration of their good fortune, a sort of timid trial of themselves in the enlarged social sphere to which the money invited them, Nell overruled her brother's more pretentious suggestions. The arrangements, of course, were left to Nell and Arthur, he having been to several club dinners. Besides, he wore evening dress habitually during the grand opera season, which he "did" for the *Index*. Nidstrom sat back in good-natured and incompetent neutrality.

Arthur was for having a caterer's man to serve.

"Would you, really?" Nell asked anxiously. "You know it's just to be a few of our friends—and Mrs. Gregg."

"Well, of course, if you think they'd think we were trying it on the dog," Arthur grumbled.

"I don't think anything of the kind," Nell retorted with dignity; "but it would be —well, rather pretentious."

"Well, what are these things for if not for pretention?"

Nell ignored this levity. "And I know Martha would feel hurt," she objected gravely.

Arthur laughed helplessly. "Of course that settles it," he said. "Or, you might have the man for Mrs. Gregg and Martha for the rest of us."

Nell was too rapt in her problem to pay attention to this chaffing. "I know I could get Mrs. Thompson's second girl's sister to wait on table," she said. "Mrs. Thompson says she does it splendidly—and I guess if Mrs. Thompson was satisfied we'd have no ground to find fault."

"Oh, certainly not!" Arthur exclaimed;

"poor, miserable scum of the earth that we are! You and Victor are throwing your money away to give a dinner. Dinners are for them that are swollen with pride. What you want is a fast in sack-cloth and ashes. Imagine giving a dinner in a spirit of true humility!" This with a wide gesture as expressing universal astonishment. "You'll never do, Nell," he added, critically. "The only way to do a thing of this kind is to take the bit in your teeth and throw up your head and go rip-snorting right through it, regardless. That's the way the nobs do. But, Lord! there isn't a snort in this whole family excepting me. Who are you going to have besides Mrs. Gregg?"

"Just Mr. and Mrs. Deere and Mrs. Wilder and Mr. Leggett and Victor and me—Mr. Gregg, of course, and you and Miss Thompson—but you'll have to take her home."

"Oh, get a man that can toddle home alone," Arthur said quickly. "Of course, I'll take her home," he added at once. "Have Miss Lilian West, and I'll take her home twice," he said, to take away what remained of the sting of his indifference to Nell's friend.

Nell's eyes smiled a little at the suggestion. "I wish I could," she said, with a kind of softness.

THE MONEY CAPTAIN

"Why not?" Arthur demanded. "Just write a note, 'Miss Lilian West, Drexel Boulevard, City.—Respected Lady: Wishing to give my brother a chance to see you without attracting suspicious attentions from the police, I hereby invite you to dinner the twenty-fourth instant. My husband works for your uncle. Hoping you are well, I remain, Yours truly, Tiggie Nidstrom.'" Tiggie being an infantile nickname of unknown etymology.

He knew that Nell took his Miss West more seriously than she should; or, at least, he suspected that it was not as serious as Nell took it to be; and he branched off at once:

"Never mind. If Mrs. Wilder is here and you cay pry Leggett away from her for a few minutes I shall have somebody. If you could only arrange to have a little scene at love-making between Leggett and Mrs. Wilder, where the other guests could peek in, it would beat the Lake Shore Drive vaudeville. Imagine Leggett melting! I suppose when he used to know her there in High Grove, before Wilder's time, he must have had some diffidence. A man can't get that hard finish at twenty. Nowadays, of course, he walks in calmly, and hangs his love conspicuously on the hall tree and cracks jokes at it."

THE MONEY CAPTAIN

To Arthur's imagination there was nothing in life that Leggett would not slap on the back; and he would have found much that astonished him in the turmoil and doubts of the big man's mind as, the afternoon of the dinner, he hurried down the worn steps of the *Eagle* office into the early dusk of a lowering October day. Rain had fallen, and the air was full of a damp that stung. Lights burned in numberless high windows. A home-going rush of men and women streamed endlessly along the wet streets, an astonishing outpouring of people that filled the broad flaggings. Cable cars with glaring headlights and clanging gongs came by in an interminable procession.

There was a resolution in the editor's figure that made little difficulty of those crowded corners where the people waited for the cars. It was as though he were hurrying in an undeviating course with his desires. Still, he felt less whole than usual. It was always so when Isabelle Wilder came in. In most relations he preserved a sort of solidarity of his own. In this affair of Dexter and the *Eagle*, for example—if worst came the newspaper might be swept away, and he could stand aside, his hands in his pockets, and say, "Well, I'm all here; you never touched me." But as to Isabelle——

THE MONEY CAPTAIN

It had happened rather oddly. Ten years before, in a country town, he being the "city editor" of the despised country weekly, and the city-editorship involving upon occasion the sweeping of the floor and carrying in of the wood for the office stove; and Isabelle being the slim, white-frocked daughter of a reclusive Unitarian minister, he had lurked behind unsuspected windows to peer breathlessly at her as she passed. Sometimes he had stammered to her. Then he came to Chicago. He thought he had gathered some capability in those ten years. At least, he had gathered assurance; he had discovered it was not for nothing that his hand was like a hammer. Presently he knew that Isabelle was married; and, after a while, that she was a widow. But he was thinking of many other things. Even after he knew that she was in Chicago, and that the way was open for him to renew the acquaintance, two or three months went by before he took the opportunity. At that time he was absorbed in the plans that were shaping to put him in control of the *Eagle*. The thick tentacles of his will were reaching after that prospective power and feeding strongly upon it. The slim, white-frocked girl of his twenty-first year was very remote from him and rather dim. Standing before her at last, he saw at once that the lines of her figure had matured; that she, too, had got a certain firm hold of her world in those ten years, as he had. That much was instantly patent, as were her very lustrous brown eyes and an alluring dimple that came into her left cheek when she smiled. She was distinctly pleasing, and Leggett was glad of that. It would have been a nuisance to go away up there on the north shore to meet her, and then to find her faded out, or dull, or fat, or frumpy. Standing before her in his completest wholeness, he found her a pretty, graceful, agreeable woman, especially admirable in the important particular of figure, of whom he could approve as the man who knows peaches approves of this one or that.

The confident man did not forget how he had dumbly groveled before this same item of femininity ten years before. It came to him with a flavor of cynical zest. He made a joke of it. Isabelle laughed and refused to believe that it had not been the grocer's daughter instead of herself—it had been so long ago—he had forgotten.

Then, with a swiftness that seemed a sort of grotesque impossibility, Leggett found himself more in love with her than ever. He jested with her more bitterly, as though he could prove to himself that it was not so;

but at the end of every device, of every profane or pious resolution, or every rage, her lustrous brown eyes shone at him, that dimple in her cheek assailed his heart. Whenever he thought of her, instantly she stood at the end of every avenue, inaccessible, tormenting him.

At his hotel, when he threshed his way into evening clothes, his thoughts of her were a smothered conflagration. But nowadays, if he tried to say a serious word, she turned it into a joke.

The house in Tremont Avenue had a festal effect, easily achieved by lighting the gas both up-stairs and down; but this, like the hurried greeting in the hall, Leggett passed over in rapt carelessness. He walked into the front room—a gleam of two lustrous brown eyes, a little, rather demure smiling and dimpling, and his world moved violently to a new key, as it always did when he came into her presence.

For the other people he had only the use of a passing amusement. As to Mrs. Gregg, it was simply an incidental item in his working fund of newspaper knowledge that she represented a social value far above any other there. This impressed him exactly as though he had known that she was a violent woman suffragist or a minor poetess. It was the tag by which he knew her place and relations. He got some amusement out of a suspicion that Nidstrom and Nell were secretly deferential to her as to a figure from a larger social world. She was a large and dark young woman, having shapeliness and comeliness in her ample and somewhat saturnine way. The breadth of her face suggested the big broker, and Leggett saw that she exercised just that repressive influence upon Gregg that Maxmann did. In her presence, as in her father's, the junior partner had the effect of nervously striving to propitiate his angry gods.

The Deeres came in last, and they brought Leggett a surprise, which from subtle causes had the taste of bitterness.

The Savonarola chair, which Mrs. Franklin had bought because of the irresistible difference between the original price and the bargain-day price, whereon he had been given a seat, commanded a view of the little hall. That was his view because Isabelle stood on that side of him near the door. Therefore he saw the entrance of the tall man and of the slender little woman whose delicately graceful head, like a flower with a silvery veil, emerged from the upturned collar of her jacket. He saw Isabelle turn quickly into the hall and put out both her hands, in which the slim gloved hands of Mrs. Deere were laid. Isabelle stooped and kissed her through the veil, and Leggett heard a quick laughing exchange of reprimands and apologies about a deferred visit. There was something lover-like about the way the taller and stronger woman kept nearer the slight one. And when Isabelle came back to the door the slight smiling that scarcely curved her lips, and the shining in her eyes, confirmed Leggett's impression that the Deeres were rather intrusive people.

He knew by that time that Isabelle had lived with the Deeres for nearly a year immediately following the death of Wilder. He had the impression that it was a year of some difficulties for her. He had never bothered particularly about it, nor about the exact processes by which the complications in Wilder's estate and the complications with the Wilder kin, which seemed to be much the same thing, had finally been smoothed away. He had found her comfortably installed at Cousin Winston's and apparently in easy circumstances. As to just what had happened before he relegated it all to the unprofitable scrap-heap of the Past — presumably she had been very uncomfortable. But he had been mixed up in some things himself that were not to be particularly inquired into. He had heard, as he would have heard that Victor Nidstrom had the measles, without exactly remembering whether the measles were something to wear, that there was some sort of far-off family connection between the dead and forgotten Unitarian minister and the unknown parents of Mrs. Deere. He believed that Deere had been Isabelle's lawyer. Also that Isabelle had been god-mother to the last baby but one. All around, he took it that honors were easy, and he was distinctly surprised at that shining in Isabelle's eyes over the slight, fragilly graceful Mrs. Deere.

Deere impressed him unfavorably. As his big hand closed perfunctorily over the slender, bloodless and inert fingers of the lawyer, he had a kind of satisfaction in feeling that he could dislike the fellow on his own account. His face was too lean and too sallow, and his black mustache was too long. His narrow forehead was too high.

When the little company reassembled in the front room, Gregg dropped on the piano-stool and struck out a few bars of a popular air.

"There isn't much music in this," he said over his shoulder, "but there may be enough to set you talking."

"If it doesn't set us distracted," said Mrs.

THE MONEY CAPTAIN

Gregg, under her breath. Gregg, with a final pass at the keys as for bravado, went over and sat meekly by the door.

Leggett found the empty seat beside Mrs. Wilder. Mr. and Mrs. Deere stood in the doorway close together. The lawyer's long, nervous hands were plunged in his trousers' pockets; his slim, round-shouldered form stooped as he talked with his wife. She smoothed the lapel of his coat with her finger, and her effect was of hovering over him in a way at once infantile and maternal. Some strands of her chestnut hair were recalcitrant to the comb, and strayed down on her delicate cheek. Perhaps from these straying strands, perhaps also from some other touches, she had a suggestion of being not quite ready, of having come hastily and unprepared, and with her this air of unreadiness was an added charm as though it asked you to take her informally. She had a short upper lip and a small nose. It was easy to imagine her with babies about her—to whom she was just a larger and merrier one of themselves.

"Mr. Deere doesn't look strong, does he?" said Mrs. Wilder, as though continuing an unspoken thought.

"Well, not exactly gladiatorial," Leggett admitted.

THE MONEY CAPTAIN

"Anna is always worrying about him as though he were a teething baby," Isabelle continued, with a kind of fondness, as though that were Anna's lovable folly. "Now she thinks if she can get him through the Gas ordinance business he will be all right."

Leggett looked around at her abruptly. "This Gas ordinance!" he repeated, with a wide stare.

"Yes," Isabelle replied; then, with a sudden new interest, as though an unsuspected phase of the affair had appeared to her, she asked: "What has he to do with the Gas ordinance anyway? Is it this ordinance the newspapers are saying so much about?"

Some rapid calculations had flashed through Leggett's mind. He grinned mirthfully. "Is he losing his health about the Gas ordinance?" he asked, not answering her question.

"Well, Anna seems to think he is worrying about it. What is it?"

Leggett bent his head and looked at Deere from under his eyebrows. This Mr. Deere was then standing before him in an unexpected and very odd light. Isabelle saw that his glance was derisive.

"Oh, it's a good business for an ambitious young man," he said, and his tone, like his look, was full of derision. "That's lovely," he chuckled. "Wearing out his health in his pure young zeal to get the Gas ordinance fixed up right. 'Wanted, young man of good home surroundings to take charge of a Gas ordinance. Must be healthy.' I suppose Dexter'll be putting advertisements like that in the newspapers."

"Isn't it—isn't it—perfectly proper?" Isabelle demanded, with a touch of indignation.

"Oh, immensely proper," said Leggett. "Some of our best citizens do it. Only at times it has turned out to be unpopular. Good, industrious young man!"

Again Isabelle felt a covert taunt, an implied insult in his tone and glance. She looked quickly away from him. In the sweep of indignation she even gave her head a little jaunty toss. She would not have him use that tone toward the Deeres. Who besides herself knew so well the sweetness of the Deere household? At a troublous time, it had been the most precious of places to her. Even now she sometimes had to go back there to start crocheting patterns for Esther and, especially, to get the eager, fluffy heads and the busy, soft little hands of Isa and Dick about her. It was a house of babies—three of them without counting Anna. There was a profanation in Leggett's taunt.

THE MONEY CAPTAIN

Besides, it was an outcropping of that quality in him which she feared. Among other men his effect was that of a spirited stallion among docile horses; the effect of a great uncurbed force hung on a hair-trigger, that might burst ruinously into ruthless action. He yielded her no submissiveness. The woman with some experience to make her wise looked beyond the wedding day and wondered what hold she could keep upon such a man.

In a moment her equable temper returned, and she began talking of something else, affecting not to have noticed his sneer.

When the guests left, Nidstrom and Nell and Arthur, standing together alone in the hall, in the midst of the silence that fell after the little gust of farewell speeches and calls, glanced at one another, and came down from their company attitude.

"Well, was it a good party?" Nell demanded, as she saw to the fastenings of the door.

"Certainly it was," Nidstrom replied stoutly, and yawned.

Arthur laughed. "Go on to sleep," he said. "I know Nell's loaded, and she can praise her dinner to me without keeping you awake."

Arthur went into the library and lit a

THE MONEY CAPTAIN

cigarette, and Nell sat down before him, ready to talk. Nidstrom loitered a moment uselessly in the doorway; then went upstairs, his heavier nerves requiring no sedative after the excitement of the company.

"I thought it was a success," Nell confessed, with a touch of self-consciousness.

"Oh, it was successful enough while it lasted," said Arthur, indifferently. "Of course, everything is stupid after it's over with."

"Do you find things so?" Nell asked.

"Yes," he replied, simply.

Nell gave a quick and grave up-glance at him—a slight figure huddled in the big leather chair, with smooth, sallow face, thin and plain except for the dark eyes. She was silent a moment, and then, as though it came logically from what he had said, she asked, seriously:

"Have you seen Miss West since——"

"No, not since the golf tournament," he replied; and he even then wondered whether, after all, he was not perpetrating a shameless fraud on Nell just for the sake of letting her coddle him, and of being a victim of fate in her eyes.

Telling her casually some six months before that he had met Dexter's niece at a

THE MONEY CAPTAIN

private view of some paintings—through the good-fortune of happening to know a young lady of society who was interested in literary things—and talking out whimsically some of the fancies that danced in his head around that pretty and amiable girl who was so near akin to him in the mere facts of youth and sex and mental sprightliness, and so infinitely remote from him in the other facts of her high and gilt position as Dexter's niece, and his low and bald estate as the $35-a-week literary critic of the *Index*, he had, as he soon found, laid the secure foundations of a big and dear romance in his sister's imagination. He did not know how much of her imagining was real, as it referred to his own condition in respect of Miss West. All of it was true and tragic whenever he looked at the photograph of Miss West that he had managed to wheedle the society editor into giving him. At other times, among some jolly friends, in a hardier atmosphere than that of his day-dreaming, nearly all of it was merely light comedy.

"The opportunities for seeing her are not many," he added, to Nell. "I've tried standing on the corner and exercising hypnotic control; but there seems to be something the matter with the connection. I suppose Dexter keeps her insulated. Or,

THE MONEY CAPTAIN

maybe, the mere atmosphere of his wealth and gross material success smothers my spiritual force."

"Well, there are plenty of other girls," Nell suggested, with a woman's inability to understand that there may be only one when it is a question of her own sex.

"Yes, there are plenty of others. I suppose that's the trouble. If some of the others who are as accessible as calico were made inaccessible, no doubt I'd be in love with them. If she were a type-writer girl now——" He mused over it a moment. "Maybe it works both ways. Miss Turlington says she's much interested in social problems. Perhaps if I were a workman in a jeans blouse she would consider me. I might get one of those soldering outfits and work into the house under pretense of mending the pipes. I might take Leggett along as my assistant, and while I declared myself to the niece he could assassinate the duke. We'd be married the day after the funeral, and come into the property at once."

Nell did not laugh; but only smiled a very little. Often he seemed most pathetic to her when he joked. Then, perhaps, more than when he was serious, he managed to preserve his effect of being a brilliant failure.

CHAPTER VI

In the morning the roses that had embellished the dinner-table drooped on the sideboard and moulted their leaves. Nell, in a wrapper, a little heavy-eyed, sipped her coffee abstractedly. Nidstrom was deep in his morning newspaper.

"You see, we can't keep it up," said Arthur.

The *Index*, which Nidstrom was reading, said that the Northwestern Gas ordinance was to be amended by the council, permitting the company to charge as high a price for gas as Dexter's companies charged, and that a clique of eastern men, with abundant capital, had bought the franchise and would fight Dexter.

The speculation in Gas shares, which had been lagging, then advanced to another acute stage. On Sunday the *Eagle* and *Clarion* repeated this report of an opposition company, and the *Eagle* added that the attorney-general's suit in quo warranto would soon come on for a hearing. On Monday, the quotation for Gas declined five points.

THE MONEY CAPTAIN

Gregg bubbled over with nervous, abrupt laughter. He whirled purblindly through the back room, bumping into people and apologizing. Standing before the blackboard, his hands in his pockets, his head inclined a little to one side, peering through his glasses, he felt independence drifting in to him, and his nerves titillated as though in a moment more he could make a plunge and lay manual hold upon the coveted fortune.

"You got out too soon, old man," he gurgled in Nidstrom's ear, as the secretary dropped in after lunch, lured by the spell of the big game. "Better sell a jag."

"I'll wait a while," Nidstrom answered, doggedly.

He noticed the men in the room, preserving the professional phlegm, but watching each quotation. Two stood in silent absorption by the ticker, their eyes on the tape as it unreeled, too impatient to wait for the figures to be transferred to the blackboard, and he thought how Leggett's vociferous appeals for civic virtue as against Dexter's corrupting manipulations would fall on those ears. When, in the course of the afternoon, he was called into Dexter's room, the duke seemed to him absolutely admirable. His effect of serene power, as contrasted with the clamorings of the newspapers and the

THE MONEY CAPTAIN

scramblings of the street, made Nidstrom think: "Those fellows are only the noise of the storm; this man is the storm itself."

In the suburban train on the way home he sat opposite two men whose talk obtruded on his abstraction in the interval before the train started. Both were well dressed, and the larger man, who had a big red mustache and had pushed his hat to the back of his head with an effect of recklessness, declared, with explosive abruptness, as though the confession were forced from him, "Do you know, by Gad, I dunno for the life of me how I ever came to do it! That's what puzzles me, by Gad!"

The slighter man gave a quick upward glance from the corner of his eye, and Nidstrom could see a movement of the muscles of his mouth as though he were repressing a smile; but he said nothing.

The big man edged a little nearer and laid his arm over the back of the seat in a more confidential way, as though moved by the necessity of explaining it.

"Because, you see, I was afraid of that damn Gas all the time," he went on earnestly. "Yes, sir, I was afraid of the damn stuff all the time, and I made up my mind"—here he doubled a great fist and laid it impressively on his companion's

THE MONEY CAPTAIN

further shoulder—"not to have a thing to do with it. Why, Lyman comes to me three weeks ago, and wants me to buy Gas, and I knew good men was buying it; but I wouldn't have a thing to do with it—was afraid of the damn stuff, you see. And at that time I was dead right on wheat. Then, you see, the wheat got a little against me, and here comes Dodson wantin' me to buy Gas—Dodson and Lyman, by Godfrey!—and I took a little of it, you see, against my judgment, thinkin' to get even on the wheat. I was afraid of it all the time, too, but knowin' these men was in, and other good men, and it came to me straight as a string that some aldermen was buyin'—Hell!" He broke off with explosive inconclusiveness, and passed his hand over his chin and sighed. "Then, of course, I kept gettin' in and gettin' in, buyin' on a scale—scale! Hell! But what puzzles me is," he added, with his former gravity, "how I ever come to get in so deep when I was afraid of the damn stuff all the time."

The smaller man twisted his mustache to brush away a smile. "Well, the restaurant is doing pretty well, ain't it?" he asked.

"Yes," the big man answered, apathetically, "the restaurant is all right—if I get this settled up." He pulled himself together.

THE MONEY CAPTAIN

"Oh, I'll get it all settled up," he added, more confidently.

The train started, and the noise drowned their talk, but at intervals Nidstrom saw the big man double his great fist and lay it on his companion's shoulder, and in the slackening of the train at 47th Street he was explaining very earnestly, "You see, I was afraid of the damn stuff all the time!"

Nidstrom imagined him going home to tell his wife, in the same state of dazed resentment, about the catastrophe which had overwhelmed them so undeservedly. It was another segment of that big and dark and complicated region in which Dexter's influence was so mighty. It occurred to him that to all these little, grasping figures, who in spite of their pettiness made so large an effect in their day, Dexter was the only great man, because his power was the only sort of power they could realize.

He purposed telling Nell of the man's talk, partly, as he almost confessed to himself, because, hearing this man, he had thought how it would have been if he had gone home to tell Nell of a loss instead of a winning, and to present the reverse case to Nell would sharpen his own satisfaction in his good fortune.

But, as soon as he got in the hall, Nell

handed him a note from Dexter. It read simply: "Please come over here as soon as you can. I wish to see you."

"I've got your dinner all on the table. You must eat before you go," said Nell, gravely.

Summonses to Dexter's house had come before, though infrequently, and Nidstrom had long got by the stage when any unusual motion on the duke's part touched his apprehension, when it brought sharply up, as by a sort of automatic connection, a general sense of Dexter's power to harm him. A possible dismissal no longer came to his mind, and the accession to his fortune helped him to a tolerable degree of independence in that respect anyway. Still, he hesitated a little over the suggested dinner. It was already 7 o'clock. The duke might be waiting.

When Nell said, answering the hesitation in his eye, "You mustn't think of going without having your dinner—the idea!" he thought how very important his wants and tastes were in that tiny world on Tremont Avenue, how other things must give way to them, how large and domineering a figure he was there, and how very inconsequential a matter it was to Dexter whether he had any dinner or not. The thought may have

THE MONEY CAPTAIN

strengthened his inclination to wait. At any rate, he went into the dining-room with Nell and Tots.

It was not far from his house to Dexter's, as the mere walking of the distance went, and the journey was something like a cut through the strata of society, as money measured its relations. An idea of the figure that he cut in his house and in Dexter's was in his mind as he climbed the broad steps to the fortress-like porch and rang the bell. He had been in the house several times, and the man who opened the door managed to signify a sort of household knowledge of him, by a slight unbending of facial muscles, without in the least compromising his dignity. Nidstrom knew the baronial aspect of the long, oak-cased hall. As one of the ducal retainers he was suffered to find his way alone up the wide stairs and to the room in the second story where Dexter had received him before. The second story hall had, of course, as much as possible the effect of a different house as compared with the hall below. The room which he entered by an open door was spacious and rich, but the only hint of its distinctive use was in a broad table encased in rosewood down to the greenish velvet carpet. Beyond the table there was a wide window, made of many irregular

THE MONEY CAPTAIN

panes of thick, dull glass, set in lead, reaching to the floor. Dexter sat on the opposite side of the table, next the window, and a tall, shaded electric lamp threw a circle of radiance over the table and over his figure. As on his desk at the Gas office, there were many papers before him, and the spot of busy litter showed the intrusion in the great house of the ceaseless and multifarious financial schemes whence came the flow of gold that supported the establishment.

Nidstrom's foot made no sound on the thick carpet, but Dexter seemed to be aware of him, for he looked up as the secretary approached the table, and nodded. The nod was a recognition of whatever slight character of host he may have conceived himself as taking on. At the Gas office he never had time for greetings, but always plunged at once into business. To Nidstrom there was nothing slighting in that. With him, too, it was business, and he would have dispensed with the nod without offense.

Dexter motioned to the chair beside the table.

"You know Deere, the lawyer, don't you?" he asked, as Nidstrom sat down.

"Yes, I know him," said Nidstrom.

"I'd like you to take this to him," said Dexter. He picked a stout, thick envelope

THE MONEY CAPTAIN

from the table, and as he held it in his hand the secretary could see that it was unaddressed. "You'll find him in his office. I'd like him to get it as soon as possible."

"Yes," said Nidstrom, simply.

"I'm sorry to bother you," Dexter added; "but nobody else was at hand, as it happened. There's so much blab in the newspapers just now that I don't like to have anybody do anything outside of my own people."

"Oh, I can do it as well as not," Nidstrom hastened to say. "That will be all?"

"Just give it to Deere; that's all. I wanted to know that it got to Deere, and that no outsider had anything to do with it. Of course, I don't intend to take up your evenings; but it happened there was nobody else this time."

"That's all right," Nidstrom assured him again. "It won't take long anyway." He got up, slipping the package into his inner coat-pocket, and buttoning his coat.

"Much obliged," said Dexter. He nodded again, and the bearded line of his lips relaxed in a slight smile. His manner throughout had been quite simple and business-like, exactly as it usually was in the Gas office.

Nidstrom perceived that he had been

intrusted with a confidential mission of importance. It would be easy to draw a sinister inference in respect of it; but he chose to put that suggestion away from his mind. Dexter trusted him entirely, and as he went from the room he was under the influence of a glow of loyalty toward the duke—such was the effect of Dexter's quiet air of mastery and command, of his attitude of poised, assured power.

Stepping into the hall, Nidstrom nearly collided with a pretty girl, in a trim, snug street-dress of reddish hue. The girl's plump little body was inclined forward. She was running and kicking out her foot at a small, woolly dog that snapped at her skirts. Her face was aglow with a kind of childish delight as she teased the snapping little bundle of wool, and Nidstrom halted abruptly, confused at stepping into this odd picture. Not long before he had been in Dexter's room at the Gas office when Miss West came in, so that he knew who she was. The dog, without any hesitation, took him into the play, and made a dive at his trousers' leg, and the girl looked up into his face with a brilliant smile, and gave him a little nod of recognition, with no more compunction, as it occurred to Nidstrom, than the dog had shown. As the little animal darted

THE MONEY CAPTAIN

back for another dive, she stooped with a swift and graceful motion and caught it up in her arms.

"Rip is dreadfully familiar," she said, with perfect assurance, and she turned down the hall, holding the dog in one arm and pulling at his woolly ears.

Nidstrom went down the stairs smiling, amused and pleased at the fleeting bit of innocent comedy in that great and rich house, side by side with the strong and dark figure of the duke. It impressed him agreeably to think of Dexter, the predatory and sinister, tossing handfuls of gold to this pretty, lively, amiable girl, and watching her play with them as one watches the gambols of a kitten. At any rate, there was nothing like miserliness in Dexter's character. Howsoever he got the money, he spent it with an open hand. Nidstrom had never seen Mrs. Dexter, but he knew that her life was a long interval of waiting for health. At infrequent periods, she received at her splendid house. Then for months she would be at a sanitarium.

The picture in the hall glowed in his mind as he crossed the lighted streets up-town and entered the marble tunnel that led to the elevators in the Bar Building on Washington Street. There was little traffic in the

THE MONEY CAPTAIN

elevators at that hour, and he ascended to the fifteenth story in an empty car. A pressure of his arm against his left side assured him that the package was safe in his pocket. The ground glass panels of the doors which he passed showed dark, but there were some glints of light in the one, near the end of the corridor, with Deere's name on it. The lamps in the front room were unlit; but the door to one of the two inner rooms was ajar, and a long wedge of light came thence. At the sound of Nidstrom's step and the closing of the outer door, Deere instantly appeared in the doorway to the inner room. It struck Nidstrom that the slight frown on the lawyer's face was an effect of nervousness.

Through the inner door, opened further to give egress to the lawyer's figure, Nidstrom caught a glimpse of a fat, blonde man, with bushy mustache, sitting in the inner apartment. This man, turning his thick neck, looked over his shoulder with a kind of provisional belligerence, and Nidstrom recognized him as "Polka Dot" Simpson. The Polka Dot was an historic and flourishing establishment on South State Street—two stories and a basement. Leggett said in the *Eagle:* "If anybody can show Mr. Simpson another profitable form of depravity he will add another story or build an annex." A

THE MONEY CAPTAIN

procession of dazed and despoiled men, sometimes with bloody heads to go with their empty pockets, wandered from the Polka Dot to the police station and made their futile complaints. Some of them went so far as to identify a culprit from among the "ladies and gents" for whose refreshment, as the white-letter sign on the windows announced, the ground floor of the Polka Dot was maintained. In that case Simpson procured bail—at customary rates. Five years before he had retired from the city council. "It's got so," he said to the reporters who sought his reasons, "that a decent man can't afford to stay in politics. The newspapers blackguard him, and it hurts his business. I'm out of it for good."

Nevertheless, Mr. Simpson's name had frequently been connected with matters of a political nature, and the *Index* had dubbed him "Bribery Broker," without being called to account.

As Simpson looked over his shoulder, another figure peered dimly from the shadows of the inner room. Nidstrom, in the mere glance which he permitted himself, saw only a bushy beard and a shock of hair.

Deere came forward at once, saying, with a thin gloss of hospitality, "Oh, is it you?

How d' do?" and he took, hastily, the package which Nidstrom handed.

"Yes, much obliged," the lawyer added emptily. For an instant the two men hung in an embarrassed pause. Then Nidstrom made an awkward ducking of his head and turned away. Deere at once went into the inner room. As Nidstrom closed the outer door he had a bare glimpse of Deere standing in the inner room, the package in his hand, and of Simpson rising with a kind of expectancy.

CHAPTER VII

It was only as Nidstrom was going down in the elevator that a related perception of what had happened formed in his mind; and he turned away from it with disgust. He even felt a touch of resentment toward Dexter. "It was going too far," he told himself.

But, after all, why not he as well as another? They were all only so many rods and blocks in the big machine that the duke contrived and operated, each used with a kind of superhumanly impersonal election for whatever purpose in the general plan seemed best to the engineer. The secretary even got an effect of himself as something quite divested of volition and responsibility, as though the only account that he need give of himself was: "Piece Number So-and-So of Dexter's Engine."

He felt almost reckless as he came out on the flagging and stood looking up and down the street. He pretended that he was in a hardily aventurous frame of mind. The street, so familiar by day, was almost more strange to Nidstrom under its night aspect than an unknown thoroughfare would have been. The electric signs of the theaters had a dissolute suggestion. Some stairways and doors, so dull and unobtrusive by day, blazed into prominence with lanterns and transparencies, hinting to him of that mysterious world which begins after dark and disappears before daylight. He stared at this interdicted world with a kind of brazenness until a passing woman looked at him, smiled a little, and swerved toward him in her walk as though to speak to him. Then he turned abruptly and hastened to the corner and across the street. It was only on the opposite corner that he dared pause to look back. He saw, with relief, that the woman had disappeared.

The exciting touch of that scene in Deere's office, like a sudden glimpse into a sinister world, imparted a quickening to even his steady nerves. He walked aimlessly down the opposite side of the block, and hesitated on the corner even at the risk of being again put to rout.

Across from him, gloomy, forbidding, loomed the huge and dingy cube of the City and County buildings. Thither he turned with a new, tentative purpose. In spite of the glare of lights opposite, the broad

THE MONEY CAPTAIN

expanse of broken, uneven flagging about the base of the public buildings seemed saturated with the shadows of the vast, unlighted, oppressive pile of stones. Polished faces of granite caught uneven reflections of the theatrical signs. Far in the darkness of the gloomy windows, set in their deep stone recesses, dimmer replicas of the opposite lights glinted and glimmered—all with an effect of making this huge, silent, dark cube, set in the midst of a city of light and motion, seem more forbidding and somber, more sinister and derelict.

Nidstrom walked on to the Washington Street entrance to the City Hall, and stepped into the long, tunnel-like corridor stretching from street to street and lighted by a row of arc lamps in its low roof. An air and effect of imperial dirt and decay assailed him from the dingy walls and battered columns. At intervals along the corridor, beside the door casings, and at the entrance to each elevator car stood a capacious iron receptacle, fashioned like a shell and filled with sawdust. Each receptacle held a day's offering of cigar stubs and of the more offensive leavings of the sovereign, tobacco-chewing majority. Around the bases of the shells was a nameless litter of shots that had missed the target. The elevator cages were of the oldest pat-

THE MONEY CAPTAIN

tern, battered, nicked and grimy. As Nidstrom's cage ascended, the conductor leaned forward, and, with nicest precision, spat between the edge of it and the floor abutment. The cage ascended slowly, giving serial glimpses into dim, waste spaces of empty corridors floor after floor. And on every floor, at every point of vantage, stood one of the shell-like receptacles, with its heap of cigar stubs and its stained sawdust, so that the stranger might have thought this curious utensil an official emblem of the city.

In the north corridor on the top floor the glass panels of several guarded doors gave glimpses of the packed council chamber, the view being of the legs and coat-tails of the back row in the lobby. Two or three policemen moved about with a comfortable air of being at home. At the end of the corridor a winding iron stair ascended, and on the landing at the head of the stair several other policemen lounged and gossiped sociably. The broad door to the gallery of the council chamber, opening from this landing, disclosed a mass of humanity packed on a short flight of steps and filling the whole view. Nidstrom hesitated. But a policeman assured him cheerfully:

"Plenty of room; reserved seats a little further along."

THE MONEY CAPTAIN

The man's eyes twinkled jocularly, and Nidstrom, edging into the pack, heard his voice making some comment at which his companions laughed. The secretary supposed the remark was a sarcasm upon his show of reluctance; and he perceived at once that his presentable linen singled him out to the policemen as an alien to that scene.

The short flight of broad steps led to a wide aisle running along the back of the gallery. Nothing was visible of the council chamber itself save the ceiling. The view in front consisted wholly of a strange ragged frieze of packed heads and shoulders. It struck Nidstrom that the heads ran mostly to odd shapes and sizes. Many of them were badly set off with tousled hair. The collar just in front of Nidstrom had sprung away from the band of the shirt, leaving an interstice of weather-beaten neck. It was for the most part the trampish crowd that one sees at police court. Frequently the warning voice of a policeman sounded: "Hats off, now!"

The long and dense pack which filled the aisle was in continuous commotion. A man, hardier than most, pushed a determined and disastrous way through it to a better view point. Another, with an uncommon sensitiveness to the hot, heavy air, reeking with

THE MONEY CAPTAIN

the fumes of tobacco, desperately edged his way out. Once in a while a policeman plowed through with majestic indifference to obstructions. Here and there a man performed the difficult feat of smoking; the action of his elbow, as he raised the cigar to his mouth, abrading neighboring ribs.

Very slowly and patiently Nidstrom worked forward until by stretching on tiptoe he could look over the shoulders of the few men in front of him and gain a patchy glimpse of the floor of the chamber. The gallery sloped sharply down from his feet, its seats filled with spectators whose effect was exactly that of the spectators in the aisle. Below, behind the curving rows of desks at which the members sat, ran a polished brass rail, and the space behind this rail was packed, but with spectators of different appearance—mainly well-dressed, and looking on with an air of familiarity. The curving rows of desks faced a platform. Over the tall chair on this platform stood the city's shield, surmounted by a large red eagle. The tall chair itself was occupied by a man of compact frame, whose features were indistinct to Nidstrom, partly because of the distance and partly because of the cigar smoke that floated up to the eagle as the chairman lounged easily in his high seat.

THE MONEY CAPTAIN

An invisible member under the edge of the gallery was speaking with a rich brogue, and with a vehemence which far outran his machinery of expression.

"So phat's the use, Mr. Chairman; I say [very earnestly] phat's the use—phat's the use—phat's the use [with a tremendous burst] of makin' enny long story short, as the gentleman fum the nint' su'gests?"

A great guffaw interrupted him.

A member at the right shouted: "There's too much noise!"

The chairman rapped with his gavel.

The invisible member: "Therefore, in dooty to my constit'ents; in dooty to—to—to our may'r; in dooty to this city, I vote,'Aye.'"

Other members spoke. A strange medley of accents arose. The debate was thickly punctuated with points of order. The member at the right insisted that there was too much noise. Members walked about the enclosed space, leaning familiarly over desks, holding consultations, exchanging cigars. The air grew hotter and heavier.

Near the center of the chamber a burly member whose snow-white hair was clipped close to his fat head arose with ponderous unsteadiness and began talking in thick, uncertain tones. His bulky frame swayed threateningly. Now and then he made a

THE MONEY CAPTAIN

grotesque gesture. One moment he bellowed unintelligibly and the next his voice sank to a muttering sound. Nidstrom could not understand what he was saying; but his condition spoke eloquently. He had great difficulty with his words, and he spent some seconds in a vain attempt to enunciate "eligible," which persisted in getting started as "egg-il——" or "edge-il."

"Vote! vote!" cried other members; and "Point of order! Stick to the subject!"

The speaker raised his voice in a thick bellow: " 'M talk'n' 'bout civil service!"

The member at the right: "Mr. Chairman, make him stick to the subject. Civil service ain't the subject!"

The speaking member, aggrievedly: "Well, w'at th' 'ell is the subjec' then?"

The chairman finally made him sit down. He floundered into his seat, and for ten minutes he kept up a vengeful volley of, "Stick to subjec'! Stick to subjec'!" as other members spoke.

A swift, rasping voice, rich, like a good many others, with hints of Ireland, arose in front of the chairman.

"Aw, there goes O'Toole," Nidstrom heard a man behind him say, in a tone which implied that O'Toole was, after all, what they had been waiting for.

THE MONEY CAPTAIN

Craning forward and stretching up, by the unasked aid of the shoulder in front of him, Nidstrom managed to get a glimpse of an arm flourishing oratorically; then of a bushy beard and a shock of hair. It was the figure that he had dimly seen in Deere's inner room. The recognition touched him with a little prickle of apprehension. He felt the man next him pushing against his side with a bent arm. Glancing around, he saw that the man was looking at the floor as though he had lost something. Pressing hard the other way, Nidstrom made a little space. The man opened his mouth. An appalling splot sounded from the floor. The man wiped his beard with a dirty hand and nodded amiably to Nidstrom, as to say that the favor should be returned when it came his turn to spit.

Nidstrom struggled resolutely back to the door, and so to the elevator and the outer air, where he took a long, refreshing breath. The night, even with the jangle of the city's lights and sounds, seemed blessedly clean and serene compared with that saturnalia of dirt and disreputability at his back.

As he walked over to take the train home that scene in the hall of Dexter's house came back to him—that secure air of luxury; that gay, pretty girl. He knew well enough

THE MONEY CAPTAIN

that the wires which moved this scene of reeking and riotous uncleanliness ran to the strong hands of the man whom he had left on Drexel Boulevard; that the splendid house, even that girl herself, were in a way a blossoming from this muck-heap.

"It's a very fertile dirt anyhow," he said, with melancholy humor, to Nell.

CHAPTER VIII

Rousing in the morning, Nidstrom's first thought was of that scene in the council chamber. He opened his eyes a little to the familiar, sanctuaried peace of his bedroom. He heard Nell's voice, low-pitched, in the alcove where Tots slept, and the child's piping treble. A minute later there came the quick patter of bare feet on the carpet, and the baby appeared at the edge of the bed, his yellow curls in a fluffy aureole about his rosy face that was shining with a mischievous smile. The mite gave a mischievous gurgle and began climbing into the bed with an energy of purpose that reminded Nidstrom, still only half awake, of a cherubic pirate boarding a helpless ship. An instant later the soft little body was snuggling close to him.

When he roused again Nell was standing over him, fully dressed, tickling his nose with the end of a folded newspaper.

"Lazy men folks!" she said, under her breath.

Nidstrom reached for the paper. He saw

THE MONEY CAPTAIN

at the head of the first page, in thick black letters, "Boodlers Win Again," and the sublines of the scare head told of the amendment of the Northwestern Gas ordinance, permitting that company to charge as much for gas as Dexter's companies did, under circumstances which the newspaper declared to be infamous.

That saturnalia of degradation came back to him. His wife stood over him smiling, her morning brightness suggestive of a wholesome flower. Tots had fallen asleep, his chubby little face mellowed in that repose to a seraphic innocence. This scene appeared to Nidstrom as though projected against the background of that council chamber where not even the caryatids under the gallery were innocent. Yet in a way he too had his economic life in that dirt and degradation. He thought again of High Grove—that simple freshness, that air of repose. There, he supposed, it would be possible for a man to have his whole life as clean and innocent as his home.

Dressing, he only glanced through the headlines of the article in the *Index*, which Nell had brought him. He knew in a general way what it would say; he had read it so often before. The same offense, the same pitifully futile clamor over and over. It

THE MONEY CAPTAIN

lighted no fire of indignation in his mind. It merely made him feel a sort of accustomed shame. It was just one more iteration in an endless series—the typical sturdy young lady with her "I Will" motto regularly despoiled over night and regularly shrieking the fact in the morning; getting up a fine semblance of outraged hysteria over it—although she knew it would happen again the next night.

The *Eagle* varied the key. Its headline said, "Dexter's Hand In It." The text, however, gave only a rather dim innuendo to bear out this bold declaration. Somewhere in the account this occurred: "Mr. Polka Dot Simpson was not observed among those present, but there was abundant evidence that he would have felt quite at home." It did not attempt to say why Dexter should have been instrumental in securing the amendment of the ordinance of the Northwestern Company, which was supposed to be an enterprise inimical to his interests.

The real shock to Nidstrom's mind was reserved for the editorial page of the *Eagle*. When he opened to that page of the paper he saw first of all, in the most conspicuous position, a double-leaded leader, a column long, headed, "Dexter the Buccaneer." In

THE MONEY CAPTAIN

the first lines he saw Leggett's hand. There were no coarse words, but the article exceeded the offense of the account in the news columns. It made a comparison between the state of the old and the new type of buccaneer, and it praised Dexter in barbed terms for having found a way to reap all the material advantages of buccaneering without suffering any of the dangers and disadvantages. Continuing, it turned suddenly to Dexter's family and social position. The old buccaneer, it said, was recognized as the enemy of society; but the new was society's admiration and model. It quoted a half-dozen excerpts from the society columns of the newspapers, telling of the society affairs of the Dexters. The names of Mrs. Dexter and Miss West were reproduced just as in the original paragraphs. Kidd and Morgan, the article concluded, would expire of chagrin if they could be resuscitated to witness the vastly improved methods of the modern buccaneer. Nidstrom shrunk from the women's names in that insulting type, as one shrinks with a sense of indignant but helpless abasement from a coarse word spoken in a woman's presence.

Other faces glowered and darkened over the *Eagle* that morning. There was a glint of battle in Rose's dark eyes as he tossed the paper from him. He got into his overcoat with an air of abstraction, and all the way up town, as his *coupé* rolled over the smooth boulevard pavement, he sat back in the corner, his arms folded, thinking steadily and not pleasantly.

When he entered the ante-room of his office, presenting his accustomed air of tranquillity, he glanced at the three clients who were already waiting for him. The office boy met him almost at the door. The boy's face asked attention, and the lawyer paused, looking down.

"Mr. Dexter's in your room waiting for you," said the boy, in a low tone.

Without looking at the waiting clients Rose crossed the ante-room and went to his own room, shutting the door after him as he entered.

Dexter's coat and hat lay on the table at the side of the broad, light room, and Dexter himself, his hands in his trousers' pockets, stood by the front window looking down into the street twelve stories below. The man's appearance, with his short, thick body, his solid, bristling head stuck forward, suggested one of those squat, powerful and belligerent animals of the bull-dog sort.

Rose crossed the room and held out his hand. "Good morning, Mr. Dexter," he

THE MONEY CAPTAIN

said, with brisk suavity. Dexter shook hands, briefly, and gave an abrupt nod, and Rose, without waiting for another word, turned to a closet in the corner of the room, where he hung up his coat and hat and then carefully washed his hands.

When he reappeared, drying his hands on a towel, Dexter stood in the middle of the room, his hands still in his pockets, waiting.

Rose tossed the towel inside, shut the door, and went briskly to his chair behind the long table. "Sit down," he said.

Dexter ignored the invitation. "Have you seen the *Eagle?*" he asked, abruptly. He had turned partly away from the table, and was pacing slowly toward the window, his hands in his pockets, his head bent down.

"Yes," Rose answered, blandly.

Dexter was at the window now, and he faced that way, his back to Rose, as he asked, "Where is that fellow most vulnerable?"

Rose considered, and waited, his chin thrust somewhat forward, his head tilted back, looking at his greatest client.

Dexter turned and began pacing slowly toward the table, his eyes on the carpet. "I can get at him somewhere so it will count," he said. "I want to find out where."

THE MONEY CAPTAIN

The lawyer found the duke's manner highly unsatisfactory. Those stubbornly downcast eyes, that restlessly deliberate pacing, the repressed voice—the entire aspect of the man was somehow alien to Dexter, and puzzling and alarming.

"Is it really worth while?" Rose suggested, blandly.

Dexter dropped into the chair on the opposite side of the table. "I want to get at him," he repeated, through his teeth, and struck the table with the flat of his hand and looked the lawyer full in the face.

An inexpressible shock went through Rose. Dexter's eyes were blazing. Their whites were marked with tiny red fibers, and the under lids looked inflamed. He added an oath that came through his set, bearded lips, with a suggestion like that of the impact of a pile-driver.

For an instant the lawyer felt astonishment and grief, as though he had found the duke drunk. Dexter, the capable, the strong, the impassive, the magnificent gamester, who staked his millions and made his greatest plays without batting an eyelash or changing an intonation of his voice; the man of that splendid nerve, which was superior to every defeat; this Dexter now overcome by a horrible rage like a squabbling newsboy!

THE MONEY CAPTAIN

Words of caution, of protest, of deprecation sprang to the lawyer's mind.

"The dog! the dog!" Dexter sibilated, under his breath. "He blackguards my wife, my family!"

And suddenly the lawyer's mental attitude shifted. He looked over into that set face with its red, burning eyes. It was like looking first at a small blaze which one may extinguish, and then seeing it burst suddenly into a grand conflagration beyond control, at once subjugating the spectator's idea of extinguishing it; sweeping over his imagination and commanding him.

Rose's black eyebrows came a little nearer together. "Yes," he said, coolly, "I fancy he's vulnerable enough; I guess we can kick him out." Dexter sat still, his arm extended along the table, palpably suffering in his rage.

"He's a dirty dog," Rose added, with a mingling of sympathy, disgust and resentment.

Leggett's offense, indeed, then seemed unpardonable. Rose knew Dexter's story. The son of a clothing merchant, well-to-do, and even of some local financial renown, according to the small standards of that early day in Chicago, Dexter had married the daughter of a hotel-keeper in the Wisconsin village where he went to fish, and his father had been furious. How Dexter got a position with a little suburban venture at gas-making in which a friend of the family held an interest; the young couple's straitened circumstances; Dexter's industry in the gas venture; the first modest budding of his financial genius in a stroke that got him a foothold in a more important gas company, through a merger with the little suburban venture, had been told over and over. In the fall of '71, the couple moved to the north side. Dexter was in New York in the interests of that first gas coup. In the great fire the young wife, alone and bewildered, met with an accident which crippled her. It was the long price that Dexter paid for having been poor. Not long afterward, as the son began to emerge from the ruck to which his father had banished him, there was a surface reconciliation. Some half-dozen years later the father died, and left the son $300,000—a fortune which the son could then almost match—but he left no recompense for the blasted health of his daughter-in-law, nor for the idea in the son's mind of what the lack of a little of his father's money had cost. Three hours after the senior's death, Rose himself was permitted to read in Dexter's face an absolute contempt for the father who

THE MONEY CAPTAIN

had withheld what might have helped, and, finally, in impotent conciliation, had handed over a fortune. There was that center of romance and of tragedy in Dexter's life, and Rose could not see it grossly touched without rousing willingly to the work of retributive justice.

Ten days later an unheard-of and non-resident owner of three shares of the capital stock of the Eagle Publishing Company filed a bill in the United States court, asking for an accounting and the appointment of a receiver.

After the preliminary hearing, in which the court refused to appoint a receiver pending a further showing, Leggett returned to the *Eagle* office, a copy of the bill in his pocket. He sat down deliberately and read the bill through; getting a new and not pleasant sensation from those long tautological paragraphs, which, in legal phrase, charged one Hamilton J. Leggett with many reckless and ruinous offenses against the rights of the stockholders in the Eagle Company. It was the kind of thing which he was wont to make light of in his paper; but this particular instance did not seem altogether funny.

Deere was the attorney for the unheard-of stockholder, who had got possession of his qualifying three shares of stock but three

THE MONEY CAPTAIN

days before the bringing of the suit. Dexter's hand was plain enough in it. In fact, there was little attempt to conceal it. Leggett had no fatuously mistaken ideas respecting the duke as an antagonist in a case of this sort. He knew the long odds which Dexter's money and influence implied. But the air of battle blew about him, and he lifted to it. After all, the attack was on this bodiless thing, the Eagle Publishing Company. Possibly Dexter could overcome that; but he, Hamilton Leggett, would be left untouched. A weapon might be taken from his hand; but the hand would remain. He tossed the type-written pages aside with a touch of contempt. As though he had abandoned the *Eagle* to them, he already felt freer and hardier, as one having nothing to lose feels an accession of daring. They might strike into the air. His blows should find flesh and blood. He felt an enormous and vitriolic contempt. Why should this scullion Dexter resent his scolding? Why should the bug seek to wriggle from beneath his heel? Why shouldn't this duke lie still and take his beating like a discreet dog, and crawl off and lick his bruises in silence? He turned to the consideration of a leading editorial article which would express about that idea.

they blamed the company for the suit. They tersely told him, through his attorney, that, in fact, there were three things possible about it. Legal action might be taken — if so, they'd respect it; they might be willing, without prejudice, to compromise this suit (a company is always willing, in cases of this sort, to avoid the 'company-identification' extra's that an out-of-court settlement can bring); but, the turn of events was to be settled to a finish.

After all, the 3 more "as on this limit" saw, the Eagle Publishing Company couldn't later come overcoming that; but a Thomson lawsuit could be left unbeaten. Lawyers might be taken from baseball; but the band would return. He stared this upon his paper as it with a tinge of contempt. Although he had about slid the 'an'l to them, he deeply felt he was not aided, as we having nothing to say both in question of giving. They had arrived as he sat. "His brow should look head and bland. He felt an emotion but slightly contempt. Why should this writer screen report his candidly? Why should he stoop to wrangle from beneath y heart, W? shouldn't 't e-lake, he still coldn't sit on his — secret day, and we't in his but the term so unsilence. He turned back to interval of treating edit-orial article about would excess about that face.

121

CHAPTER IX

The name Miss Lilian West, quoted in Leggett's leader, taunted Arthur Franklin with the mortal and intolerable sting of an unpunishable insult offered to one's women folk. He sat alone in the library finishing his cigar. The newspaper, which he had not even wrathfully crumpled, lay across his knees neatly folded. His whole undenied, accepted, inevitable incompetency loomed bodily before him. He was useless, so what was the use?

He was not given to meditation. He ruminated aloud, needing the inspiration of other faces and voices to keep his mind at a light and graceful poise. When he thought alone the thoughts harried and oppressed him. His imagination, which was his friend and his escape when he talked, became his enemy and prison when he was solitary. In the matter of Lilian West, the kindly sympathetic presence of Nell and Victor helped him over to her, in his satirical and comic pose; but without those helps a gulf yawned—yawned, he told himself, because it was

THE MONEY CAPTAIN

bored. That was the trouble. The despair which confronted him was not the somber mask of the tragic muse; it was a thing with dull, weary eyes, and a grotesque face as though in the midst of a grin it had been stricken with death.

Lilian West poised on a peak infinitely remote from him. Yet, a week later, in the entrance of a theater given over to "continuous" vaudeville, at 10, 20 and 30 cents, he suddenly found himself looking at her, bowing to her, then at her side, being introduced to her two indistinct women companions.

He had been rather late at the newspaper office. Passing the door of the theater on his way home, he had dropped in merely because the lights, the idea of the crowd within, attracted him, offered him one of those escapes from Time which he was continually taking. He stood in the back part of the house vaguely interested in the scene presented by the darkened parquet. It was in the middle of the performance, and he staid only a few moments. In the gaudy entrance, glowing with lights and lined with photographs of performers, he got by a pillar and loitered again. He found a tiny, cheap pleasure, the cheapness of which he realized, from standing there in his fawn-colored over-

THE MONEY CAPTAIN

coat, brown felt hat and gloves and stick, with an affect of being a man of the night and the crowd. In its tiny, cheap way, it was something like the pose he sought—that of being at home in all places and of calmly observing. Then, near by, he saw three women who had just come from the theater, talking gayly together as they moved to the flagging. The one nearest him was little and plump, with lightish brown hair and a fine color in her cheeks. Arthur saw only her distinctly. In the moment of astonished, tremulous abeyance, all things stopped save the motion of the girl's lips as she smiled. She looked up, saw him, and stopped as though it were all by prearrangement.

He did not catch the names of the companions distinctly, and his glance took them in only vaguely. One was a girl about Miss West's own age; the other was considerably older. Perhaps it was the little embroidered cape on Miss West's shoulders that made her seem distinguished from them.

"We were bound to see the 10, 20, 30 cent show," said Miss West. "They say it's what the theater is coming to anyway, so we made up our minds to meet it half-way."

She moved a little as she spoke, and in a moment, they were stepping out on the flagging in an irregular group and walking

THE MONEY CAPTAIN

very slowly while Miss West talked. Arthur was acutely conscious of the whole environment; and he was tormented by a vain attempt to find his proper relation to it. The girl was absolutely at ease. She had a perfect effect of competence and of assurance; perhaps beyond that, a little charming touch of royalty, as though whatever she chose to do thereupon became right. A carriage was drawn up to the curb a little way ahead. He supposed that it was hers, and it helped him to subdue the overpowering, anxious self-consciousness, and to rationally rearrange their relations. After all, she was only stepping out of her frame to him for an instant, as she had done at the picture gallery and the golf tournament. In a moment more he saw the situation satirically, and became self-possessed. Loafing at the entrance of a cheap theater he meets a girl whose whim has taken her there, possibly just because it is a little unusual and tastes of independence; and to her, of course, he is simply a part of the 10, 20, 30 cent adventure.

"I think it's a very good thing," she was saying. "I don't see why the newspapers shouldn't encourage it. What a fuss they made because the 'Opera House' "—she spoke the words scornfully and glanced up at the wide bedizened glass awning from

THE MONEY CAPTAIN

beneath which they were stepping—"was turned over to vaudeville, as though it were a kind of profanation! Why, you know, they often had the wretchedest things there at a dollar and a half a ticket? And now it's really not so bad an entertainment, and so cheap that anybody can go. Why should the newspapers object to that?"

"Well, the newspapers get in free anyway, you know," said Arthur. "I suppose they resent having their privilege cheapened. They'd rather the price were three dollars."

In reaction from the nervous doubts of the first moments of the meeting, he began to feel elated and confident. So long as she made the conditions it was no affair of his, he told himself. He saw that they were passing the carriage and that she was quite oblivious to it, and if she proposed to visit a police-station, or a ten-cent lodging-house, he was quite ready.

"There may be something in that," she said, as she walked serenely on, evidently unaware of anything that needed explanation. "But, really, don't you think that the prices at the theaters are too high? You know, nearly all the things you see in the theaters—the melodramas and farces and what they call the society dramas—are just suited to entertain laboring men. But the

THE MONEY CAPTAIN

price is so high the laboring men can't go, and the people who can go are not entertained. We shall go in for the 10, 20, 30 cent, shan't we?" she called over her shoulder, to the two indistinct women who had some way fallen behind.

Arthur noticed that she accepted him in the simplest way in the world; and that, with the little touch of royalty which he found perfectly charming, she expected the indistinct women to accept whatever arrangement she chose to make.

"As part of the press, you should have it rearranged," she added.

"I will see to it," he said; "but it's too late for the Sunday edition."

They had reached the alley which bounded the rear of the *Index* building, and from the basement the strong whirl and rattle of the great presses, revolving at express-train speed, came up to them. A row of little windows, close to the sidewalk, were opened for ventilation. With the noise of the swift and powerful machinery, a strong flood of white electric light came up. It fastened the girl's attention instantly. She stopped and even stooped a little to look into the basement. Enormous ribbons of white paper ran, like the flowing of water in a cataract, into the huge machines, from which, at the

THE MONEY CAPTAIN

other end, the printed and folded newspapers dropped in a continuous shower. Walking around the presses, or perched on their great frames, were men, stripped to trousers and gauze undershirts, watching the multiform operations of the machinery.

The women looked for a moment. When Miss West glanced up at Arthur he saw, with a thrill of gratification, that she invested him with some of the suggestion of mystery and power which the scene offered.

Miss West did not offer to move on, and she asked him, with a touch either of childlikeness or of that piquant effect of royalty which he imagined in her, "Do you go down there?"

"My presence isn't strictly necessary," he replied, smiling; and then, coming into the momentary gravity of her mood, he answered, calmly, "Sometimes I go down."

"It's splendid," she murmured, "and those men——"

Whatever the question was, she did not complete it. A narrow iron stairway led from the alley to the basement. The opening was guarded by a railing of iron pipe. Miss West, standing on the flagging, had suddenly become aware, as Arthur had, of three men at the top of the stairs—evidently

THE MONEY CAPTAIN

from the press room. Like the men below, they wore only trousers and gauze undershirts. Two of them sat on the top step, their backs to the group on the flagging. The third man stood a little lower down, so that the top of the iron railing was only a little below his shoulders. His arms, very white, bare and sinewy, were folded on the rusty iron, and his chin rested on them. He had a long, dark mustache, and his curly hair was cropped close to his round, shapely head. He was looking calmly at Miss West. The low-cut undershirt bared the smooth and powerful base of his neck at the back. Arthur, encased in his overcoat, regarding this brawny, handsome, careless man as from the consciousness of a body as delicate to chills and shocks as a woman's, suffered a bad moment in which he found himself puny and tiny and inconsequential. The man's eyes were not exactly insolent; but they regarded the pretty girl, who also looked frankly at him in the moment's contact, as though, after all, with her suggestion of money and refinement she had no advantage over him with his splendid muscles; as though there was no reason, if he were so minded, why he should not walk over to her and say, "Will you come with me?"

The contact of eyes lasted only a moment.

THE MONEY CAPTAIN

Miss West looked into the basement again, then walked on, leisurely.

"It's odd that the people in a newspaper building don't know one another," she suggested, thoughtfully.

"Oh, they come and go at different times, and are in different parts of the building. I suppose they have different interests, too," Arthur replied. He felt a little irritated by the suggestion of her remark. He supposed she was accusing him of superciliousness or indifference.

At the moment a lank boy, wearing a blue uniform cap, came shuffling hurriedly along. It was one of the city editor's messenger boys, and Arthur called to him, with insincere cheerfulness, "Hello, Joe."

The boy glanced up at Arthur and the stylishly dressed girl, and dodged hastily by without a sign of recognition. As soon as he was by them, as though to show that he was not abashed, he began whistling loudly and he took on a more pronounced swagger in his shuffling walk.

To Arthur it relieved the embarrassing tension. He laughed naturally. "You see it won't do," he said. "These people refuse to be fraternal. They recognize an innate superiority and it abashes them."

Miss West smiled in a way that put them

at ease; but she did not laugh. "Isn't that always the way?" she asked. "The real trouble with fraternizing isn't in the attitude of the people who are best off, but in those who are worse off. Isn't it those people, not the best-off ones, who are always remembering the distinctions about money and position and so on?"

Arthur found the question embarrassing, because he didn't know whether he was expected to see the problem from the point of view of the upper or the lower class. "I suppose it's mostly a question of like taste and interests," he said, indefinitely. He was really wondering where they were going.

They had come to the street corner. "We came on the street-cars, you know," said Miss West, stopping. It might be a dismissal; but the cable train was a block up the street, and she did not step from the flagging "I think the street-cars are good—and so convenient," she added. "Certainly they belong with the new theatrical order. We made up our minds to that." She looked at both her women companions, as taking them to witness.

"We are used to the street-cars," said the younger of the companions, simply, as though she would not be put in a false position. Arthur looked at her more carefully. She was plain, but intelligent and with suggestions of strength in her broad mouth and well-rounded chin.

"Well, I'm used to the street-cars," he said, as though taking the opportunity she made to confess, "when I'm not walking to save the fare."

Miss West gathered her skirts to step on the pavement. "I can pay your fare tonight," she said over her shoulder at him, and instantly he stepped out beside her.

The conductor, one hand on the bell-rope, accelerated the women's entrance to the car by putting his free hand on the back of each one, as though he were handing parcels along to somebody inside. Miss West entered first, but the two others sat beyond her, so that Arthur was left a seat beside her, to which he staggered as the car started with a violent jerk. Within the half-empty car his proximity to her was given a new and heightened effect. Her little cape brushed his arm. The bloom of her cheek was intoxicatingly near. When she looked around into his face, laughing, the nearness shocked and confused him. Her smallness and plumpness gave a more tantalizing quality to the lure, and he had one or two dizzy instants, as though he were actually about to catch her in his arms and

THE MONEY CAPTAIN

say, peremptorily, "See here, you maddening little thing, I love you?"

At first his exultation was curiously alternated with misgivings and sudden abasements. But these left him, or only visited his remote subconsciousness in faint gleams. Before they left the car he was warmed through and through with the joy of her presence. Walking along the quiet cross street with her beside him and the two silent women on the farther side, he even imagined himself definitely projected into her atmosphere, really habited to her plane. As they turned into the boulevard he glanced along the row of big stone houses with an oddly serene feeling of being on a familiar footing with them.

At Dexter's house the electric lantern burned in the fortress-like recess of the granite porch. Pausing barely an instant, Arthur lifted his hat and said, "Good-night."

The three women said "Good-night," and as they were stepping up to the cement walk which led across the lawn, he was walking on. It was as simple as the incident of passing an acquaintance in the street. He walked on, still, for a moment, in the rare and joyous air of her presence. The house stood at the corner of the street, and as he turned toward Tremont Avenue, he looked

THE MONEY CAPTAIN

up and saw the three figures, Miss West last, disappearing through the broad, carved oaken front doors. As the door shut his atmosphere quickly dissolved. A little further along, he stopped on the stone walk, looking up at the side of the great house. Its many windows suggested innumerable rooms, all richly furnished, all with an effect as of overflowing with gold. The great, costly, granite-cased establishment crushed him.

When he let himself into the house in Tremont Avenue, after an hour's aimless wandering in the street, its little snug homeliness made a singularly pathetic appeal to him. He felt as though he must wake Nell and Victor and make them come down and surround him with their unaffected fondness. When he took off his overcoat to hang it in the hall he heard a faint jingle of coins in the small pocket. Reaching in there, he drew out a quarter and a nickel—the change the conductor had given him from the half-dollar with which he paid the fares on the street car. The coins brought her vividly back to him as she had sat beside him in the car, and he took them, first the quarter, then the nickel, and kissed them.

An instant later he dropped down on the seat of the hall tree, the coins in his hand, laughing dolorously. He looked down at the metal disks and imagined himself kissing them, and his sides shook with laughter that wrung his heart.

The laughter helped him pull himself together. Up-stairs in his own room he went over and examined the writing-desk in the corner with a singular interest, as though to ascertain the thing's physical verity were an important point. The desk had been there three years. He remembered very well the care with which he had selected it, and the shaded lamp, and how he got them placed in the room with a regard to the best use of the north light mornings. In the drawer lay the first half of the first act of a play and part of the first chapter of a novel and suggestions for two or three short stories. In the last two years he had now and then found the desk a convenient place to toss a collar or tie.

Now he opened it and stood for a moment in a sort of surprise at himself. A moment later he was seated arranging a pad of paper. There was no ink in the well; but he had a pencil. He wrote for a few minutes, and leaned back in a surprised and admiring pause which lasted several moments. He got a highly agreeable sense of himself, seated with that studious and literary air in the light of the shaded lamp. His first para-

THE MONEY CAPTAIN

graph nearly filled one of the small sheets on which he wrote. He felt that he had struck the note of an editorial article, replying to Leggett's attack upon Dexter's social relations. The continuation of the note, however, began to grow difficult. A hundred unbidden things obtruded in his mind. It was only about half-past ten o'clock. A strong temptation assailed him to go back up-town and see how his literary air would feel there. And he felt very tired, all at once. To get up early in the morning and continue the article—a dozen subterfuges lured him; it seemed that there was a cunning necessity compelling him to relinquish the task. Finally the girl came back to him. With a desperate gripping of purpose he bent over the desk.

When he got up in the morning he went to the desk first of all and looked at the thin pile of little sheets, neatly written and headed and lined for leads. He went down to breakfast wearing a little halo of virtuous success—which was quite useless to him until somebody else had admired it. The device by which he finally showed the article to Nell cost him a struggle with his self-respect; but he got the audience he needed.

Nell sat down with the air of doing something very important and read the article

THE MONEY CAPTAIN

gravely. As she put down the last sheet she beamed up at him. "Why, that's splendid!" she declared.

The notations for the printer impressed her mightily. She saw the article at once clothed with the imposing effect of type on the editorial page of the *Index*.

"You ought to do more of this, Arthur," she said, with a blending of admiration and sisterly reproof. "Nobody else on the *Index* can write like that. It's true," she asserted quickly, as he smiled. "You know it's true. Nobody else writes —well, like a gentleman. Of course your literary reviews interest you more. But I think work like this would give you more influence." She let him take the manuscript with a little effect of reluctance; and got up smiling into his eyes. "When it's printed," she said, softly, "I'm going to show it to Mrs. Gregg, some way; and she'll show it to Miss West."

Arthur laughed. "I might send her a marked copy of the paper myself," he said; but he did not forbid.

At dinner that night Nell kept smiling at him unaccountably. She seemed in a state of extreme, almost of irresponsible good humor, and Arthur lingered at the table after Nidstrom went to the library.

"Will your article be printed in the morn-

THE MONEY CAPTAIN

ing?" Nell asked, with an effect of eager conspiracy, as soon as Nidstrom was out of the room.

"In a day or two, I fancy," said Arthur. "Hartley glanced it over and seemed pleased with it."

"Hartley?" Nell repeated.

"He has charge of the editorial page. Of course these thing that are turned in by other than the regular editorial writers are used, when they happen to be available, just as convenience serves—that is, when there isn't a press of the regular matter."

"He said in a day or two?" Nell persisted.

"Well, he didn't say anything," Arthur replied. "Of course Richards has the final say; but Hartley seemed pleased with it. It doesn't make any difference when it's printed, you know—that is, so far as timeliness; day after to-morrow is as well as to-day."

"I saw Miss West to-day," said Nell abruptly.

Arthur stopped dandling the subject.

"It was Mrs. Gregg's day, you know, and I called, and Miss West was there. It turned out beautifully, for they talked of newspapers and Mrs. Gregg brought you in, and for just about five minutes Miss West and I had a sort of little confidential aside. She asked a good deal about you. And when she mentioned that *Eagle* thing, I told her what you thought about it. I could do it, pat, you know, because I had your article in mind. I suppose I quoted about two-thirds of it to her, and got credit for being a first-rate conversationalist. So now, you see, when it's printed, I can just send it to her myself."

Nell was leaning across the corner of the table, beaming with an air of gayety that lacked little of being explosive.

Arthur smiled, first, at her enthusiasm—but after all, the thing itself wasn't so bad. A misgiving came to him. "Of course, it may not be printed at all," he said.

"Oh, I didn't say anything would be printed," Nell replied, quickly. "I just told her what you thought, and I said sometimes you wrote editorial articles—that they always wanted you to, and when you could find time, you did."

Arthur dropped back in his chair and exploded with laughter—in which some of the merriment was an overflow from his pleasure in Nell's story. "That was lovely!" he declared. "Whenever I could get a little relief from my onerous duties my kind heart prompted me to give the poor old *Index* an editorial article!"

"Well," Nell began, defensively. Then she stopped, looking over at him merrily.

THE MONEY CAPTAIN

"I guess you're not offended because I put it that way—to her," she said, " and, besides—" gravely—"you know it's so. They would like you to write more editorials. You said yourself that Hartley was pleased."

Arthur did not attempt to reply; but, going to the library, he passed his arm around his sister and hugged her—which might be either because her simplicity amused him or for other reasons.

He had resolved to take up that long-neglected play; but for this evening of course that was out of the question. In the agreeable turmoil of his mind the solitary room up-stairs was impossible. It would be like having a celebration all alone. He would go up-town. But he stopped in the library to smoke with Nidstrom. Presently Nell came in, and their plot escaped from her. Nidstrom smiled sympathetically over it, and almost at once, without there having been time to really do anything, it was half-past ten.

CHAPTER X

The waxing of the fight between Dexter and Leggett was like the converging of two antagonistic lines in Nidstrom's mind. He detested the noisy brutality of Leggett's assault; but as to Dexter's prosperous iniquity, as to the moral anarchy in which the duke wrought, his conscience stood aloof in silent but stubborn disapproval. Like every one about Dexter, he had a certain loyalty; the duke's quality of command imposed upon him; yet he felt with the vast indefinite mass of the people whose attitude toward all men like Dexter was one of suspicion, opposition and hatred. Secretly he wished most to get away, to end all this by a simple act of desertion—especially since the unclean touch of that errand to Deere's office the night of the council meeting.

When Dexter notified him Wednesday afternoon that he would be made a director in a new company he received the notice as he would have received any other not extraordinary instruction. In the changing and combining of the corporations which Dexter

THE MONEY CAPTAIN

controlled he had now and again found himself director, or treasurer, or secretary. It was toward ten o'clock Thursday morning that he learned the name of the corporation—the Northwestern Gas Company, which was supposed to have been in opposition to Dexter. The permanent organization of this company, with directors and officers made up of Dexter's employés, was promptly communicated to La Salle Street. During the forenoon the attorney-general's suit was called for trial—and continued indefinitely. In a word, Dexter was in possession of the two points of vantage whence effective attacks were supposed to be coming.

All this had the effect of the sudden unmasking of a battery. Gas stock shot upward with the explosive burst and violence of ignited gunpowder. The Stock Exchange became a riot. At moments it was inarticulate with clamor. The quotations of Gas shares in the brokers' offices strung out in long columns that doubled back and went twice and thrice across the blackboard. The uproar, the insatiable, pell-mell, indiscriminate strife, as of a lot of newsboys over coin flung in the street, continued the next day. At the close, Friday, Gas stock was quoted at $92\frac{3}{8}$—an advance of forty points in the week.

THE MONEY CAPTAIN

Saturday morning at nine o'clock a brisk young man pasted a large sheet of letter paper, written upon in a Spencerian hand, in the middle of the glass panel to the front door of Drouillard & Company's Bank. The Spencerian writing said, "In the hands of the Marquette Title and Trust Company, Assignee."

A man who was crossing the rotunda stopped, watched the clerk, read the sign. In a moment there were three other men about him also reading the sign, and waiting, as having seen the curtain rise and proposing to witness the rest of the play. Two policemen sauntered in. One of them ascended the narrow iron stair, which, clinging to the marble wall, led up to the closed door. He took up a position, impassively, on the landing before the door. By that time the crowd in the rotunda impeded egress to the elevators, and the other policeman began, impassive and silent, to line it up so as to leave a free passage-way. An excited man rushed in and ran up the iron steps. He peered through the glass panel, and shook the knob of the locked door. The large, impassive, blue-coated guardian, his thumbs in his belt, leaned against the door jamb and watched these efforts calmly, his head a little to one side. The man kicked the door, and the policeman stepped in front of it, shouldering the depositor back.

"Aw, what's the good o' that?" he remonstrated. "It's busted; you can't get in."

"I gotta get in," the man returned, shrilly from his excitement; "I got a note due to-day." His hand reached for the knob.

"Aw, go on, now," said the policeman. "Nobody can get in." He put a brawny, forbidding blue shoulder in the man's way.

The depositor looked around as though to appeal from this decision. The stairway below him was already filled with eager-faced men, some of them with pass-books in their hands. There were two women in the pack. One of them clutched a pass-book and sniffled with a little, hysterical, moaning sound.

The policeman addressed them, in a tone of patient remonstrance.

"You won't do no good standin' here," he said. "Might as well go home. The bank's busted. Can't nobody get in."

But nobody stirred. The men on the stairway simply waited, eager, helpless, caught in the current of their catastrophe, as though after all the dreadful sign might be torn from the door, the policeman dismissed, and Drouillard, appearing at the head of the stair, might apologize for the inadvertence of the

THE MONEY CAPTAIN

shut door and invite them in to get their money.

Nidstrom, pushing through the swinging front doors happily, saw the throng in the rotunda and the pacing policemen, of whom there were now two, with wonder. He entered, his mouth a little agape. Then he saw the pack on the stair, the policeman before the closed door, and an apprehension rose slowly up and clutched his heart. For a moment he stood, in abeyant helplessness, staring. A man just in front of him, who, also, had been staring, turned to go out. His eyes chanced to meet Nidstrom's, which helplessly questioned him.

The man laughed and swore in a breath. "Well, their bloomin' old bank is busted good and plenty," he said. "They've got my fifteen hundred; let 'em go to the devil with it." His chubby and ruddy face broadened in a maledictory grin, and he pushed his way out.

Suddenly Nidstrom gathered himself together. "Let 'em go to the devil with it," he repeated, comfortingly, and went on to the elevators.

A moment later Drouillard Jr., weary-eyed and slow, but clean shaven and trigly dressed as ever, came into the rotunda. He gave only one quick and shifting glance at the crowd on the stair and in the rotunda, and he made a little, quick catching of his breath. He found the three conspicuous, blue-coated figures which his shifting eyes had taken in rather comforting, and he started hastily across. The only egress to the closed bank was through a little private door off the elevator-landing on the next floor. As Drouillard approached the open elevator cage, his head slightly bowed, he became aware of another figure, coming over from the left and making for the cage—a short and burly figure, thick-necked, in an overcoat of which only the top button was fastened, so that the skirts spread apart, and the man's ungloved hands were thrust in his trousers' pockets.

The paths of the two figures converged at the door of the cage and Drouillard gave way, politely, with a little duck of his head, saying, "Good morning, Mr. Dexter."

"Good morning," said the duke. His dark eye calmly surveyed the thronged rotunda and the crowd on the stair, and came back to the man beside him who had broken against his strength. "Fine, sharp weather," he said, as though neither of them could be thinking of anything else.

"Tiptop," said the banker, urbanely. He bore no malice. Luck had favored Dexter

THE MONEY CAPTAIN

that time; but it did not enter his conception that the game was played out so far as concerned himself. He would fix up this little difficulty and try conclusions with Dexter again. His mind was under the merciful paralysis of the shock of his failure and he was like a man, who, receiving a mortal hurt in battle, struggles up to his feet with an apologetical smile for having fallen, and tries to go on with the fight. On the second floor Drouillard stepped out, with another little duck of the head to Dexter, and as the cage shot upward Dexter's dark eyes rested on the pudgy, well-clad figure hastening to the private door. The intervening floor shut off the view. The duke's lips moved as in a slight smile for an instant. Then his mind reverted to other things, which were coming to it continually as water to a mill wheel. When he entered his own office the broken banker was definitely behind him with the host of other things over and through which he had made his way.

Down in the rotunda a man near the head of the stair said to his neighbor, with a touch of excitement, "There goes Dexter."

The man whom he addressed—a middle-aged, spectacled man with a homely, good-humored face—strained outward, peering.

"You missed him," said the first man. "He just went up in the elevator."

The other man, who had a pass-book clasped in his hand, glanced at his neighbor with a kind of good-humored regret, as one used to missing desirable things.

"I'd like to a seen him," he confessed. "He must be a wonder."

The first man shook his head sagely. "He's a bird, and no mistake," he replied admiringly.

The edge of Dexter's big stroke bit into many a side. The usual chorus of wails and objurgations arose from the vanquished. Those who were unhurt stood aside and frankly admired the victor. Two other doors were closed—doors of small importance, so that in their cases the failure was a sign for contempt, Drouillard's being large enough for respectful treatment.

Gregg, coming to the office wan and furtive, heard the word passed in the back room, "Drouillard is broke." He crept hastily to his own little stall, midway between this back room and the front office of the firm, and closed the door, with the instinctive preference of the small animal for its own hole to die in. Sitting in there, huddling miserably before his desk, he felt rather than heard the ponderous, farmer-like tread

THE MONEY CAPTAIN

of his father-in-law coming along the aisle.

Maxmann entered deliberately, and shifted the catch in the spring lock so that it would hold against any attempt at intrusion from the aisle. He closed the door, calmly lifted the chair from the corner of the little apartment, placed it at the end of the desk and sat down, facing his son-in-law. These preliminaries were conducted with the unhastening coolness of a surgeon preparing to remove a limb.

The cold anger which Maxmann felt for the slender, waiting figure before him was of a dangerous quality. This giggling, jumping feather-weight whom he had never permitted to take an independent part in the firm's business, whom he had treated like an office boy and thought of like a boot-black, had lost him a fortune. To the big broker it was as though a fly which he had watched with a contempt too complete to suggest a defensive attitude had suddenly stretched up and bitten off his hand.

But the business proposition came first. How deeply was the house involved? How was it secured? What would it lose? He proceeded to get the information with impersonal directness, as though Gregg were not involved in the matter.

THE MONEY CAPTAIN

"How much is Drouillard short here?" he asked; then, "What have we got to show for it?" and he added with a cool touch that was something beyond insolence, "I want the facts this time, understand, all the facts; no more lies."

Gregg did not even flush at the imputation, He was too completely broken to resent it. He answered the questions.

Maxmann made some computations on the back of a letter that lay on the desk, first glancing at the letter to see if it were prudent to mark it. He went over the calculations with deliberation, drew a heavy pencil line under the final sum and looked up at Gregg.

"You was in with him on this deal, wasn't you?" he asked, coolly.

"No, sir; no, sir; not a bit of it," Gregg answered quickly, not stopping to wince from the lie. "You know how he's always traded here—" his manner became excited. He lifted a lean, clenched fist to strike the table in emphasis of the further disclaimer. "I tell you I never—"

The fist was about to descend; but Maxmann said, with deliberate disgust:

"Oh, hell!"

Gregg's fist faltered weakly down to his lap.

THE MONEY CAPTAIN

Maxmann looked over at his son-in-law a minute through his large-bowed spectacles. He wished it were not injuriously forbidden to put one's heavy boot-sole on things of that kind.

"You was in with him, wasn't you?" he repeated.

"No, sir," Gregg iterated; but quite feebly.

"Like hell you wasn't," said Maxmann with a ponderous contempt that was all the more crushing because it expressed itself absolutely without passion. "If you'd thought the deal was all right you wouldn't a covered it up the way you did. You was in with him. I always knew you was a fool," he added, judicially; "but I never knew you was a thief. You've lost me a hundred thousand dollars."

For the first time he showed irritation. Mentioning the amount of the loss seemed to stir his temper. The very frailty of the thing against which his anger was directed inflamed him.

"Damn you!" he exclaimed, in a loud, full voice.

For an instant the anathema was terrible to Gregg, and he broke under it as under a blow. He sank back in his chair, his lips apart, and stared at his father-in-law. It was like the descending of a dreaded bolt. It seemed to brand him and cast him out. Then, to his empty ears, came the quick, metallic clicking of the telegraph instruments in the next stall and he straightened up a little and looked anxiously around as though he feared the clerks would overhear.

Maxmann may have thought of that, too. His small, bright eyes in the midst of his broad, flat face twinkled angrily, intently, at Gregg for a moment. Then the senior partner became self-possessed.

"Maybe you can do something to help me out of this," he said. "Then, I suppose I'll have to pension you—or lock you up. I'll see. But keep out of the way now."

He went out, leaving Gregg like the miserable urchin who is told to stay until the parent returns with the switch.

CHAPTER XI

Nidstrom went through the day in a kind of stubborn resentment, and it was only as he approached Tremont Avenue that the catastrophe really overcame him. As he climbed the steps to the little porch his mind quailed in a void remorse. The loss of their money was so useless and so cruel. In a helpless way he felt it quite impossible to present the thing to Nell, as though that would make it irretrievable and as though, without her knowing it, he might some way manage to go back to day before yesterday and withdraw the money. But probably she already knew of the failure from the evening newspapers.

Nell met him in the hall, gravely, and took his overcoat as he got out of it and passed her hand over the velvet collar.

"How damp it is!" she said. "You ought to wear something around your neck."

"Yes, it is damp," he admitted dully.

She hung up the coat; then, simply, passed her arm around him with a mothering touch.

THE MONEY CAPTAIN

"You mustn't get sick on top of our other troubles," she said.

At that caressing touch, the bitterness of his mood relented and he began at once:

"I should have drawn the money. I knew better than to leave so much with Drouillard. I was going to draw it in a few days and buy some bonds; but I've been busy at the office, and I thought just a few days longer wouldn't matter." He went on that way. He even remembered the man whom he had overheard in the train trying to explain away the hurt of his disaster. He knew that man was ridiculous; but for all that he couldn't help explaining. It would have been so easy to save the money; he had lost it by such a trivial inadvertence—as though there were a comfort in that.

"Don't you think we'll get any of it back?" Nell asked dubiously.

"Oh, I suppose not," he admitted with a sigh. "I guess he's been gambling a long time. They say he was short fifteen thousand shares of Gas. A failure of that kind is generally hopeless." That confession helped him. At any rate the worst had happened.

"I don't see how a man dare take other people's money that way and speculate with it," said Nell.

"They seem to dare," said Nidstrom. He

laughed briefly. "I suppose it's only a sort of dying by the sword, because we lived by the sword. We made money in the Gas speculation and Drouillard lost it for us in the same speculation."

"The paper says some of the depositors are going to prosecute him," Nell suggested.

"Well, I don't know but they ought to—some of them," Nidstrom replied thoughtfully. They had moved down the hall and now entered the dining-room, where they found Tots industriously enlarging a hole in the lace curtain. Nell reproved the child in a kind of aside and sat him in his high chair, while she said to Victor: "It seems to me all of them ought to prosecute him. It was wrong."

"Is I a bad boy, papa?" Tots appealed, tearfully.

Nidstrom, leaning from his chair, put his big arm comfortingly over the little shoulders and hugged the child's head to his breast. At that moment the child's dependence was infinitely sweet.

"Well, I don't see how I could very well prosecute Drouillard for doing about what I've been doing. Of course if it was money I had worked for I should feel differently."

"The money was ours," Nell replied stoutly.

THE MONEY CAPTAIN

"It seems that it wasn't," Nidstrom replied, with an attempt at laughing. "We never really had it, you know. Gregg gave me a check and I handed it along to Drouillard and Drouillard passed it on to somebody else. I suppose there's never any real possession among gamblers; the stakes simply circulate around. And it looks as though we were all getting to be gamblers. It seems to be the clearest and swiftest exemplification of the theory that we can't really own anything for ourselves but can only keep it in trust a little while. I wish the tenure of the trusteeship were a little longer," he added with another brief sigh.

Nell smiled a little. "Well, dear, it's too bad," she said, "but we're as well off as we were before."

"No, we're not," said Nidstrom. "Then we hadn't had the money and lost it. We're that much poorer now. That's the worst of it. The ups really help nobody—this money of ours, I suppose, is now lost among Dexter's millions—while the downs count fearfully."

Nell thought of it a moment, and it touched her indignation. "I don't see how a man dare take other people's money that way," she repeated. "It's stealing."

"Yes, in a way; but I suppose he couldn't help it."

"You mean the temptation was too great?"

"Not exactly the temptation," said Nidstrom. "Temptation is only at the beginning. After a man gets far enough along in a thing he belongs to it; he has to go on. This Gas speculation, for instance—after Drouillard got well into it, I suppose there wasn't a time when he could have got out. The only hope was to go on—and there wasn't much hope in that as it turned out. Oh, it's the rule here," he added with a flash of antagonism. "What can you expect? With everybody scrambling and clutching, even if you're lucky enough to grab something you must take the chance of somebody else grabbing it away while you're reaching for another piece. It's part of the plan. The only thing," he added with sudden resolution, "is to get away; get into a different atmosphere. Think of that country place! How insane and squalid all this seems beside that!"

He looked at her with a question; but even in her downcast eye he read the same silent, uncontentious opposition to his plan, and he said nothing more.

Arthur came in presently, and commiserated them and blamed Drouillard.

"It's one of the chances of the war we're fighting in," Victor insisted; and when

THE MONEY CAPTAIN

Arthur declared that Dexter should make up the loss to him, he said, with a laugh, "I don't know but I'd be justified, as things go, in taking that much of the funds of the Gas company if I could get hold of them."

When the men came down to breakfast the next morning Nell appeared quite serene and even merry. She beamed over at Arthur now and then and finally he caught the hint, with a leaping of the heart, and left the table abruptly.

"In the library, on the mantel," Nell called to him as he went out. "It's printed—in the paper this morning," she said in an undertone, joyously, to Nidstrom. "Of course," she added, as though she would not be happy in Arthur's success while Victor suffered, "it doesn't bring back our money; but it's good in its own way." She looked past her husband's face, smiling a little, and Nidstrom saw that she had already put away the loss of the money and was reveling in her quiet way in Arthur's romance.

"Well, it will be some satisfaction to him, whether the girl pays any attention to it or not," said Victor indulgently.

"But she will pay attention to it," said Nell confidently. "Any woman would," she added, as though to authoritatively stop any contradiction. She became more thoughtful. "Of course nothing may come of it," she admitted; "but she will not forget it. It's beautifully written, and it takes just the right position, the right attitude. She will appreciate that." She dreamed away again, presenting Arthur, modestly victorious, to the admiring Miss West.

She expected Arthur to return, deprecatory but smiling, with the paper; and she anticipated the effect which his editorial article, duly in print, would have on Victor. Arthur tarried, however, and in a few moments she went to get him.

She found him humped over in a chair, the opened paper lying on the floor, while he stared gravely down at it.

Stooping, surprised, she picked up the paper. It was opened to the editorial page, and there was Arthur's article.

"Did you read it?" she asked, surprised and at a loss.

"Did you read it?" he repeated.

Nell glanced at the caption, "A Public Man's Home," just it had been on Arthur's copy. Then, slowly, vaguely aware of a mysterious disaster, she settled down on the leather lounge and read.

The article started familiarly. Arthur's phrases were there. Leggett's attacks on a prominent business man were referred to.

"The *Eagle's* diatribes have their place—that is, the barrooms where they are mostly read. But not even the dullest and grossest of the peculiar *clientele* to which the *Eagle* appeals will accept its invitation to visit upon a man's home the opprobrium alleged to be due his public acts. Home is a providential devise whereby the best that is in every man is treasured away from the worst." In a moment, however, a new voice intruded, clumsily. "But," said the article, "what shall be said of a man who lays open his very home to attacks of this kind?" So throughout the remainder of the three-quarters of a column, the whole purpose of the article was perverted, and the effect was not exactly an endorsement of Leggett's attack; but an air of treating it as a perfectly logical and inevitable result of Dexter's course. The article even went further and spoke scornfully of the giving way to the craze for notoriety and display which led some men to make their family's social affairs subject for public exploitation; as evidenced by the excerpts quoted in Leggett's leader—some of which had been clipped from the society column of the *Index*.

When Nell finished the article, speechless

THE MONEY CAPTAIN

for a moment with grief and indignation, she knew that Leggett's offense had been outdone.

"I might have been prepared for it," said Arthur, under his breath, as Nidstrom came in. "I heard at the office to-day that Hartley was short of gas and had lost $20,000. Of course he's furious at Dexter, and he changed the whole thing."

The size and significance of the disaster projected itself suddenly upon Nell's bewildered mind. She did not forget the large part she had taken in preparing the mine.

"Oh, Arthur," she wailed, on the verge of tears, and she caught his listless hand between her palms.

"Stop it! Stop it, now!" Arthur cried peremptorily. "What difference does it make? Not a rap. Of course you know as well as I do," he added more quietly and fondly, "that this business never was real. It was just a fancy. I'll make myself another fancy. It don't make any difference, Nell."

Nidstrom had picked up the paper and glanced over the article. He tossed it away again. "It's a shame," he said; "but, then, it's just another turning of the dice."

CHAPTER XII

The failure of Drouillard gave Leggett an opportunity of pointing out Dexter's corrupting influence in the world of business; but he improved it only incidentally. Another and far bigger opportunity seemed shaping to his hands. He was often a party to snug little councils held behind carefully closed doors. An impulse of silent but violent pursuit, emanating from him, touched mysteriously along subterranean ways. Simpson, the ex-alderman to whom these ways were as the path home, half felt that inimical presence in his burrows, with the alert uneasiness that a rodent might feel over dim signs of an enemy in its earthy runways. It came finally to an open note of alarm that sent Simpson to defensive action.

When the ex-alderman, walking doggedly from the railroad station, according to the direction of the agent, turned into St. Germain Avenue, he observed its suburban aspect and swore at it under his breath. The rather pretentious dwellings, set back from the clean cement walks, had an

THE MONEY CAPTAIN

effect of spaciousness as compared with the packed houses of the city. The light of the gas lamps shone into the bare branches of the oak and maple trees. The deserted verandas, the brightly lighted windows, with drawn shades, the air of roominess and retirement may have had an attraction for another. But Mr. Simpson, noting that the street numbers could not be read without going across the lawns, was disgusted.

"A devil of a place to find anybody!" he muttered with vehement contempt.

He approached two doors with a certain provisionally defiant air, only to be confronted with a number other than that he sought. The third door had no number, and when he rung the bell and asked for Mr. Deere, the young man who answered him, peering out from the lighted hall at his fat figure, told him that Deere lived two doors beyond. He tramped across Deere's porch therefore with some certainty. A little girl answered his ring. When he asked for Mr. Deere she held the door open, innocently leaving him free to enter. As Simpson stepped into the lighted hall the little girl called into the interior of the house:

"Papa! Papa!"

In a moment Deere appeared through the portiere on the left of the hall. As the lawyer appeared his face expressed an urbane readiness to become hospitable; but at sight of Simpson it swiftly darkened into a frown. Without any greeting he came over and stood before his caller.

"What is it, Simpson?" he asked, and there was a touch of petulance in his voice.

Simpson glowered up at the forbidding face and growled back angrily, "It's the devil and all, that's what it is. You—" he saw the child, lingering with an air of elaborate abstraction near the portiere. "Where can we go and talk?" he demanded, under his breath.

Deere glanced about and yielded with ill-humored reluctance. "Come up-stairs," he said, and led the way without looking back at Simpson.

When Deere lit the gas in the small room up-stairs where he did his thinking at home, Simpson took off his yellow overcoat and tossed it on a chair with a kind of rough challenge as though defying Deere's frostiness to daunt him. Then he sat down without removing his hat. Both men were angry.

In another place they met on the democratic footing of business. But Deere, in his own home, looking over at the fat, blonde figure with its diamond stud and its ineradicable flavor of the saloon and the race-track,

THE MONEY CAPTAIN

was moved by a distaste which he took no pains to conceal.

"I don't like your coming here, Simpson," he said coolly.

"What the devil do I care whether you like it or not?" Simpson retorted. Down town he and Deere got on very well; but out here the ex-alderman also had his distaste.

Deere stopped abruptly, with a kind of shock, and stared, speechless, at his caller.

"Good Lord! Do you think I come out here because I was hankerin' for your society?" Simpson demanded, in a louder voice. "I'm just as mighty willing to keep away from you as you are to have me. I'll tell you that. Good God! I can't afford to be seen around with you, Deere; I've got a reputation to keep up."

The words, like so many whip lashes, instantly subdued Deere's vexation. He was quite cold and calm. Anger was perfectly useless. He sat down.

"Well, what do you want?" he asked. "I suppose, after all, you wouldn't have come if it hadn't been something important."

"Now you're shoutin'," Simpson replied, somewhat mollified. "I believe somebody has squealed," he went on, coming at once to business; "somebody has gone and blabbed—a whole lot of lies, of course, about

THE MONEY CAPTAIN

a talk with me and you, maybe, and some attempts at corruptly influencin' and so forth." He spoke calmly and looked the lawyer hardily in the eye.

"What makes you think so?" Deere asked. "But I've talked with nobody," he added quickly.

"No," said Simpson; "no more have I. But I think somebody has told something with me and you in it. Anyhow I got the tip the *Eagle* thinks it's got something of that sort. I don't know just what it is—but I didn't care to send a messenger; and there might be somebody out to see you, see? and you might be told that I'd said something."

"Of course it's right I should know." Deere hesitated a minute. "I'm obliged to you for coming. Have a cigar."

Simpson took the cigar readily and lighted it. He bore no malice. Deere was thoughtful a moment.

"It might be rather nasty," he said. "But, bah! those newspaper sensations—you know what they amount to. Nobody can do any harm—except you." He looked over at Simpson as he said it.

"Or you," Simpson replied, returning the look.

Deere gave a little laugh. "A little reflection will show you how my interest lies," he said lightly.

"Well, what do you think of me?" Simpson demanded.

"Oh, that's all right. Of course I know where to find you. And I guess you know where to find me. In fact I don't know anything."

"No, neither do I," said Simpson. "These damn newspapers," he added, "and people who want to reform things—and get a few fingers into the pie themselves. If they'd mind their own business and had any business to mind, there wouldn't be all this trouble."

Deere looked darkly into his cigar smoke a moment. "Well, they don't accomplish anything," he said. "Do you think the *Eagle* knows anything?" he asked abruptly.

"Oh, I don't know," Simpson replied, impatiently. "There's Bueloh—he's half cracked anyhow. He might have tried to tell 'em something. Suppose they have got something. Nothing ever came of that sort of thing before, and nothing ever will unless somebody is fool enough to weaken."

"No, nothing ever comes of that sort of thing," Deere repeated. "Of course, it's a nasty kind of mess to have your name mixed up in—but nothing ever comes of it." The phrase comforted him.

After Simpson had departed he sat smoking and frowning, and telling himself that nothing ever came of those newspaper sensations. In a bad moment he wondered, with a prickle of apprehension, whether Simpson might not betray him; but he fortified himself as to that by remembering Simpson's valuable reputation as a promoter of bribery. The enterprise in which he was engaged would win, as it had a thousand times before, he told himself, because the strongest forces in the community were its allies in one way and another, and its beneficiaries in one way and another. Personally he would greatly prefer some other avenue to money and position; but this was the way that actually offered itself to him; and, after all, the goal was the only thing. He didn't like Simpson's coming to the house; but there must be some unpalatable incidents, and even if he were watched what could any one make of that?

Not much could be made of it, of course; but the report of Simpson's call, duly coming to Leggett, in the obscure and wonderful phraseology of the detective, fed him with its precious little. Sitting in his den at the newspaper office Sunday afternoon, he read

THE MONEY CAPTAIN

it over, with a thin pile of type-written sheets taken from the same locked drawer. Among these was the copy of an affidavit made by an alderman, describing the attempts of Simpson to bribe him to vote for the amendment of the Northwestern Gas ordinance. An interview with Deere was set forth. How lucky that he had got that clew to Deere! It had been the nub of the situation. Leggett replaced the papers and locked the drawer with a pleasant sense of strength coming to a focus. Of course it was not unprecedented. Other cases of that kind had been presented to the public. There would be denials and counter charges. Probably when it came to the state's attorney's office everybody in the net would wriggle out as others had wriggled out before them. But Leggett did not care so much for that. He knew that he could convict Dexter in public opinion; in that arena the *Eagle* would be victor. Affairs had been working very well of late in spite of Dexter's lawsuit. He had attracted the interest of some men with money. With the prestige of this stroke against Dexter he could, perhaps, get them to the point of taking over the capital stock of the company and giving him a secure tenure of control, in place of the present

THE MONEY CAPTAIN

provisional arrangement. The prospect unrolled before him—a renewed *Eagle;* a secure and full-bloomed Leggett. As he prepared to leave the office he felt a kind of affection for the establishment. Even the wobbly desk and dingy den evoked his fondness.

If only the woman were amenable to any sort of force! But she stood beyond him. He felt that. Her lustrous brown eyes laughed with security; her dimpling cheek maddened him unconcernedly. He felt it a kind of elemental wrong that any woman should be so tempting and so inaccessible.

It had grown very warm for February. The little snow had mostly melted and the ground and air had the tepid sogginess of early spring. The streets, as Leggett came down from the *Eagle* office, looked quite deserted. The stretches of granite pavement were bare of vehicles except for the occasional cable trains and a rattling cab or two. Innumerable windows in the towering dingy walls were dead. The few people moving over the wide flaggings at the bases of the huge buildings, made the empty reaches look all the more forlorn. The town might almost have been a vast and fantastic formation of rock, with deep intersecting cañons, in a forgotten place.

THE MONEY CAPTAIN

Although he did not forget those typewritten sheets his mind turned mostly to Isabelle Wilder, and he expanded to the invitation of the warming air. The sap of his big body responded to the inspiration of that misplaced spring. He felt a strengthening of power. As he waited for the cable train, looking leisurely up the street, many big and fine accomplishments that did not become quite definite seemed near and possible to him.

CHAPTER XIII

In the white macadamized North Shore avenue that sloped down to the water, Cousin Winston's house was the last toward the lake. Mrs. Wilder herself, answering Leggett's ring, let him into a hall that seemed to have no definite bounds as against the double parlors on the right or the hall sitting-room on the left. The broad, low doorways were scantily hung with draperies giving an effect of variable suggestions rather than fixed bounds. A fire flickered pleasantly in the hall grate, for down there the breath of the restless lake modified the air.

Leggett came in rudely aglow from the fresh air. There was a moment, marked outwardly by a little one-sided smile, when his desire hung about Isabelle in abeyant, helpless bewilderment, so that he might have pleaded, "You see, if I have everything that I want besides you, I will have nothing." In that same moment of full contact of the eyes, when each stepped from the other's dream into the other's presence, Isabelle might have confessed—

THE MONEY CAPTAIN

They shook hands, very briefly. Leggett dropped his coat and hat on the window seat. Each recovered swiftly from that leaning instant in which they had been so near together. For Leggett's part, on second thought, if this young woman thought there was anything in making a monkey of him she was at liberty to do her best. As for Isabelle—he never got far away from that hardy, impudent attitude. Ah! if he would even make her a pretty little speech. She had her reservation. Leggett had his grievance. Standing before this woman, whose red waist and duller, belted skirt neatly and trimly encased her so that the charm of her vivid face and the charm of her fine figure were at once focused to his hungering senses, the man was aware that fate was taking liberties with him; that to make a woman so alluring and to put her beyond his reach where she could laugh at him amounted to a special trial, devised for him beyond the trials of ordinary men. It was a sneaking and prejudiced fate that took him in his one unarmored spot. A sense of this kept his mind in a singular irritation and engaged his pride, so that at times his attitude toward her was as much as to say, "Well, bring on your rack; do your worst."

THE MONEY CAPTAIN

He sat down in the capacious willow chair before the grate, and Isabelle sat on the bench along the side of the stair-casing, near, yet far enough away.

"I believe I could almost catch some fish off that pier down there to-day if I had on a hickory shirt and overalls and no shoes," said he.

"Did you think of that?" Isabelle asked quickly, lending her teeth and dimple. "Why, when we came home from church I thought how I'd like to be back in the parsonage yard at High Grove and dig up a flower bed. I have a mania for digging in the dirt when it gets warm. I thought it was undignified when I was seventeen."

"Now that you're twenty-seven and it is undignified, I suppose you don't care."

"I don't care, but I'm not twenty-seven."

"Well, I'm glad you're not back there in High Grove then; for I should still be thirty-two."

"Really, shouldn't you like to be back there, even for a few days?" She turned her head a little to one side and looked at him merrily. "What would you do if you were put back there?"

Leggett looked into the fire thoughtfully for a moment. Then he said deliberately, and seriously, "Well, if I were put back

THE MONEY CAPTAIN

there deviling in the High Grove *Gazette* office, and deviled more or less by everybody about the establishment, on my three dollars a week or five, with my clothes that never quite hung together, I think I should look around for something large and heavy, something, say, about as big as the moon, and I'd try to lift it up and let it drop where it would do the most harm."

"Oh, but you've succeeded!" the woman protested quickly. His speech hurt her. It was that rough, belligerent, intolerant, headstrong scorn. What should she be able to do with that?

Leggett looked at her with a smile of indulgence. "Well," he said, "I no longer have to give my landlady an order against my wages to pay my board, if that is what you mean."

"You know you have succeeded," she persisted. "You have become a Personage. You have a newspaper."

"Ah, wait till I do have!" He affected to speak more lightly, but the watching woman saw a passing rigidity of some muscles about his jaw, a slight lowering of his eyelids. After all this man was a power; his force was known and taken account of in that big mysterious world of affairs. In spite of his youth men had to reckon with him. The idea appealed to her, for a moment it even made her a little humble; and the little glimpse that he had just given her of his plan there, like a confidence, caught at her heart.

"You will have it all your own," she said, or asked, rather, smiling a little, quite seriously and speaking with a kind of softness.

Leggett looked over at the pretty woman who was looking seriously into his face with that candid admiration. Perhaps nothing else could have flattered him out of his self-reliant reserve.

"I mean to have it and to make something worth while out of it," he said. "I rather feel that I owe that much to those years on the farm and to those years in High Grove when I was doing a boy's work at six feet one." He paused a moment, looking into the fire. "Just for myself, as it stands now, perhaps I shouldn't care so much," he added, slowly. "But I suppose unless I really do something that is worth while I'll never get over the taunt of some things that happened to me earlier." He glanced up at her with an odd sort of apologetical look, and she saw that it was a confession from his depths. It moved her very strongly.

"Yes," she murmured, before she got a

THE MONEY CAPTAIN

full breath; "I know you will make something fine out of the newspaper."

"I hope to," Leggett replied briefly; "if I get it."

"And you think you will get it—for your own?" she asked quickly. She did not propose that rapport should be broken.

Leggett was thoughtful a moment, and twisted at his close cropped reddish mustache. "Well, it takes some money," he said. "I haven't got it; but I'm now carefully working up a little explosion which I hope will land me on my feet."

Mrs. Wilder waited a moment for him to continue. She was deeply interested. "A —what you call a sensation?" she suggested.

"What I call a great public service," Leggett replied, "and what my envying competitors will call a sensation, I hope."

"And then you'll own the paper all yourself?" she asked. She was at a loss; but it interested her and she had a sense of being on a new footing with Leggett—serious, confidential and friendly.

"Well, perhaps the connection isn't so direct. A newspaper is mostly valued for the harm it can do, and if I tear up a large chunk of the earth's surface hereabouts I can get some men to see that the *Eagle* is worth having," said Leggett. He too felt

THE MONEY CAPTAIN

that they were getting on a new footing, after girding and jesting at each other for so long—a footing next-door to that one he wished.

The dimple came in Isabelle's cheek and she folded her arms tightly, as though hugging herself. "How Guy Fawksey!" she exclaimed. "Tell me all about it. I should burst with importance if I knew beforehand."

"I don't want you to burst."

"Well," she said, and her teeth and dimple helped her, "I'll guess and you tell me when I'm hot or cold. That is," she added with a sudden misgiving that straightened her face, "unless it's a scandal."

"It's the most scandalous kind of a scandal," said Leggett; "but there's no woman in it."

She smiled again. "It must be great to be around on the inside of things that way and know what's going to happen."

Leggett grinned. "From a feminine standpoint I suppose it is."

"And I've been trying to encourage you," she said reproachfully.

"Well," he admitted, gravely, "it is great once in a while—when you see somebody who's occupying a front seat in the grand stand, with the properest and most imposing air, and you know that in a couple of minutes the police are going to come along and throw him out."

Isabelle's eyes fell abruptly to her lap. It was again the intrusion of that big, brutal combative force which she half feared and altogether hated; from which she shrunk as a sensitive person shrinks from a man in an irresponsible rage. Dimly she began to perceive the conclusion toward which his talk had pointed.

"Is that your public service?" she asked, in a little lower voice; "to throw somebody out?"

Leggett for his part perceived the sympathetic scruples which had arisen in her mind, and he felt a vast contempt for them.

A sudden premonition, the half-outlined shadow of a warning that had long lain fallow in the woman's mind, came to her.

"Is it," she asked, hesitatingly, looking at Leggett, "something about the city council?" Rather oddly, and without seeing a logical connection, she was recalling distinctly the derisive and insulting glance he had cast at Deere.

Leggett's combative contempt answered promptly and hardily. "Yes; some people you know may be interested in it."

THE MONEY CAPTAIN

He saw instantly that he had made a mistake, politically; but the words were said. He stood upon them for an instant in mere instinctive hardihood, looking coolly over at her. Then very swiftly the situation presented to him a brand new and somewhat perilous facet and he squared his mind belligerently at that.

It was of course through Isabelle that the first clew to Deere as the connecting link between Dexter and Simpson had come to him. He had found it convenient and had taken it. In the first place he was right; he was the law and Deere was the crime. In the next place he had taken the clew as a man whom Fortune cannot impose upon takes any favor at her hands. In working out the case he was so securely intent upon the end in view that as other disclosures were made he fairly lost sight of the unimportant starting point. In so far as he had thought of it at all, incidentally and carelessly, it had appeared rather humorous that the clew should have come through Isabelle.

But just now, with that handsome, desired face directly before him, the red lips parted, the brilliant brown eyes widely staring at him with fascinated directness—why, the woman came into the affair with a force which he had not reckoned upon.

THE MONEY CAPTAIN

"You mean Deere?" Isabelle breathed helplessly.

She knew what the newspapers said about bribing members of the city council and she supposed it was very abominable of the members to be bribed. As the newspapers never said, she did not know exactly who did the bribing and so far as she had any impression in that direction it was that the bribe-giving side of the transaction was on a far superior plane. The mysterious hint that he had dropped about Deere at Nidstrom's she had never pursued. It was repugnant to her and she had let it alone, with a kind of stubborn but unreasoned determination to live above Leggett's vulgar insinuations. But now the idea of something sinister, disgraceful, ruinous, came darkly and alarmingly to her mind, although she was still far from having put all the bearings of the case together.

"You—are going to publish something—" she asked.

The pretty, startled, sympathetic woman thus looking her helplessness presented to Leggett the threatened intrusion of some unhealthy sentiment, some puling, feather-brained, Miss Nancy squeamishness. Secretly he was irritated and impatient over it. He thought it not at all worthy of Isabelle.

THE MONEY CAPTAIN

Since it was Isabelle, he would try to show her a much larger and deeper significance in the affair. He saw also that he had told her a great deal. He shifted his position in the big chair and the movement brought him closer to her. "Of course I mean Dexter first," he said; "but Deere is in it incidentally." He brushed his hand over his hair and the act suggested to the woman the man of broad activities. It was like seeing him at work over his editorial desk. "He's been bribing the council for years," Leggett went on gravely, presenting his case. "He's been walking over people's necks for years. Because he's been full of fight and unscrupulous and cunning, everybody has been afraid of him; nobody dared stand up before him. He's had his way in everything until he thinks he owns the earth and can do whatever he pleases and nobody will dare do more than make a few faces and call a few names. Well, I'm not afraid of him. I'm as ready to fight as he is. I despise him." Isabelle saw that he was not boasting; that the strongest and boldest of other men must reckon with this man who came so often to see her. "In a way," Leggett went on, "this thing is what I've been working up to for years. It gives me my opportunity. Some ten years of my

THE MONEY CAPTAIN

labor are invested in it and I don't think I'm a man to give up my own very easily."

It was taking form to Isabelle as something inevitable, a working out of some unknown but infallible law against which nothing would avail. Her lips quivered slightly and she still looked at Leggett with that intent helplessness.

But the man with fatal determination went on piling up more breastworks. "It's the law. The thing is worth doing for its own sake and I would do it for that. I would do it," he added without blinking, "if Deere were as much my friend as he is yours. Somebody must do these things at times or there will be no law. As to what you told me about Deere, it may have hurried the affair along a little. I don't deny that it did; but in the end it would have been the same. I would have found him out, or somebody else would."

"Did I—was it what I said to you—" her words failed; her heart swiftly sank away.

"As I say," Leggett answered hastily, "that may have hastened it a little; but in the end it would have been the same."

She was beginning to recover from the shock of the idea. "But you can't use what I told you in that way," she protested with a sort of bewilderment.

THE MONEY CAPTAIN

Leggett smiled a little. "How can it be helped?" he asked. "The knowledge came to me. Nothing could take it away." He really wished to deal indulgently with her weakness. "Besides, you are making too much of Deere's part in it. He is necessary as a link holding the affair together, but it won't really be so bad for him. Simpson, the go-between, will be sent to Joliet. Deere will probably be indicted, but he can scarcely be convicted on the evidence we now have."

"Indicted! Convicted!" She spoke with an effect of leaping back from the words. She had not thought of that before.

Leggett was finding her very trying, but he wished to be indulgent. In time she would see the sane side, which was his side. "Well, bribing aldermen is different from playing tiddledewinks, you know," he said. "If you make a misplay you get more than being politely laughed at. You go to the penitentiary. It's right, Isabelle," he added gravely.

The enunciation of her name came nearer to being a tender word than any other he had ever given her in seriousness. Oddly, that was the last straw which quite crushed her. It brought her intimately into the affair on his side, as though he were carrying her along bound and helpless to a participation in this ruin of the Deeres. At the moment she felt his ponderous tenacity as something against which she could scarcely struggle, so that all she could do was to clasp her hands in her lap and stammer:

"Oh, you mustn't do this! And on account of what I told you! Why, I lived there a year. They are my own people—and more. Those two babies are just my own. It couldn't—anything like this couldn't come through me. Don't you understand?"

Leggett glanced away; but his jaw looked very square.

"If babies counted highway robbery would be a safe pastime," he answered harshly. Her very emotion had its sting for him. He had shown her his side of the case, in a confidence such as he was little used to giving; but all her sympathies, all her solicitudes were for the Deeres. She took no account of him. "It was Deere's place to think of the babies," he said.

"But you can't help thinking about them," Isabelle persisted. "You can't! And about Anna. Nobody could." She saw the two round little faces, gravely wondering over this calamity, like innocence in the presence of death. With a quick motion she put her

THE MONEY CAPTAIN

hands to her face. "They would come and reproach me in my sleep if their father—"

Anger began to glow hotly in Leggett's mind. This silly insistence upon the mere sentimental view was exasperating. She might at least do him the courtesy to listen to his side of the case and not keep crying continually about these Deeres. He felt that she was making a scene; that she was using her emotions to trap him. It required an effort to hold himself in hand. "Nevertheless, it's right," he said doggedly, and stood up.

"No! It isn't right!" Isabelle dashed out the words from her very helplessness. The ring of her own voice encouraged her. She had an instinctive feeling of taking her stand on the ground of woman's tenderness and sympathy as against this masculine, brutal, inexorable law and logic. As Leggett arose the imminence and cruelty of the disaster as well as the intimate nearness of the potential help against it appealed to her. She sprang up as though she could detain the fleeting opportunity, as though her sympathy could interpose a valid check to the impending ruin.

"It isn't right," she repeated earnestly, as though she were arguing the point with him. She faced Leggett with a sole des-

THE MONEY CAPTAIN

perate intent to win for Anna and the children if she could.

"You won't do it," she went on convincingly. "You can't when you think about it. You are too big and strong. You can win in another way. What would success be worth to you if you spoiled that woman's life?" She intertwined her fingers, her hands being near her breast, then stretched out her arms, her palms extended and her fingers still intertwined—a mechanical motion like that of person in pain.

She stood quite close to Leggett, intent, excited, looking up into his eyes. She had never been so close in any such attitude. A faint perfume from her waist came to his nostrils. As he stared down some fine threads of hair at her temples and at the side of her neck looked intimately near as never before. For an instant the circle of her extended arms seemed subtly to invite him.

In that instant while his mind was still hot with resentment toward her the whole mass and bulk of his passionate desire fused in a helpless tribute to her physical lure. The pathos of his love summed itself in a kind of irony in the moment when she most mocked him by indifference to his success and by groundless sympathy with this cheap fellow Deere. Her excitement communicated to his veins, so that he had a passionate wish to beat down this stubborn tormenting prepossession in favor of Deere; to seize her in his arms; to say with command, "Don't think about Deere. I'm worth twenty Deeres. See how I am committed to this affair. Consider what it will be for me to do what nobody else has done—to crush Dexter, to drive him out, to drive out the council gang. To whom, besides you, would I have told as much? Admire my battle!"

But as before, he held his anger by a strong effort and squared his jaw doggedly. "I can't help it," he said.

"Oh, but it's just you who can help it!" she cried. "You know you can do it or not do it just as you please. Really, you know it is just for your advantage, your success, as you call it, that you are sacrificing them—and me. Yes, sacrificing me. It was I who told you. It is my secret, my confidence, that you are using in this way. For old times' sake, at least, you ought not to do that!"

It was too atrocious! She accused him of sacrificing her dishonorably! A burst of rage swept over Leggett's mind.

"I won't do it; I promise you," he said abruptly.

He spoke almost coolly, although it was the explosion of his wrath and scorn. He

THE MONEY CAPTAIN

tossed her the promise as, at that instant, he would have tossed her his world, out of a scorching contempt which would settle the score between them at a stroke at any cost. He could put it in a word. This woman whom he had loved took from him his opportunity, his years of work, his manhood, his belief, his independence, and handed it all over to her friends. She gave him away as a slight token of her regard. He counted for as much with her as a puppy that she might make a present of. The triumphant escape of Dexter, his own explanations to his allies in the bribery quest, danced indistinctly before him a second after he had pronounced the promise. This hollow fool with the dimple did it! The thing reached down to the pungent and bitter spring of his strength and pride. She should have valued him more than any other man and she valued him least. Well, he could value himself in the great price that he paid for having loved her. Let it go at that. He could pay more than any other man and walk out without so much as batting an eyelash. Since she insisted upon it, let her take her payment and go to the devil with it. He esteemed her less than a bit of crumpled paper to be tossed into the wind. A wicked prompting came to him, as having paid the bitter price

THE MONEY CAPTAIN

—his was not a chivalrous attitude. He put out his arm.

His hand barely touched her waist before she took a swift step aside. Confused for an instant, as though an awkward mistake had happened which must be politely ignored, she said quickly and emptily, "I felt sure you wouldn't when you had thought of it."

Leggett could fairly have laughed. Certainly! She took it as a polite five-o'clock-tea favor! She had no idea of owing him anything.

"All the same it was generous of you," Isabelle added futilely. She began to perceive more clearly, as he silently reached for his hat and coat, that he had yielded her nothing; that he had only flung her the boon she begged.

He would not answer her; she was not worth so much.

"Good-bye," he called with a mocking cheerfulness; and went out hastily.

The door closed behind him. Isabelle saw him pass along the porch and down the walk. Half mechanically she brushed the back of her hand over the spot on her waist that he had touched. Finally she sat down in the willow chair, leaning her head against its back. Cousin Winston's house seemed singularly empty.

CHAPTER .XIV

From the moment Leggett left Mrs. Wilder until he stepped from the cable car at Washington Street the whole series of scenes and incidents was jumbled and indistinct, as to a man who is violently dragged a distance while he struggles furiously with his captors. His eye took in the face of a pretty girl at the car barns where he changed from the electric car to the cable train. Presently he noted a stream of people coming from the Turner Hall concert on North Clark Street. He got up in the car to give his seat to a woman. But these were mere flying, disconnected, incidental bits mechanically caught at during the tempestuous ride.

Standing on the pavement, as the cable train pulled away, he looked emptily at the dreary street. Lanterns and transparencies showing the way to some restaurants and saloons were already alight. The electric letters of the theatrical signs to the east blazed dully in the daylight, with a moth-eaten effect because some of the little lamps that formed the letters were dead. There

THE MONEY CAPTAIN

was a singular confusion in his will. Without thinking about it he had been going toward his hotel on Twenty-Second Street, his mind mechanically running the trail of habit—but, my God! why go there?

Why go anywhere? The completeness of his disaster rushed upon him with new torment. He had lost the woman; he had lost Dexter. The two got together in a mad way and smiled at him superciliously. He turned toward Wabash Avenue, where he would find the car to take him home, and paused, looking uncertainly about him; and it was a sense of appearing ridiculous to the few people on the street rather than a decisive turning of his will which made him face about abruptly and walk to the *Eagle* office. There at least he was in his own hole, where nobody could see his bruises.

In his dingy den he shut the door with a crash, which was a sign that he wished to be alone, and dropped in a chair. The bewildering rage still beset his mind and he whirled around and around in it helplessly. In one tormented moment he thought of writing to Isabelle and withdrawing his promise. But almost instantly he flung aside that suggestion. He had tossed her the boon she begged. To beg it back would be more intolerable than anything else, especially since she put it on that ground of what he owed her. In another moment he helplessly felt her lure as she had stood before him with her hands clasped, and the irrevocable loss of the woman seemed worse than the other losses. What did Dexter matter? His imagination fell into the sinister conception of Dexter snugly taking over to himself his defeat as to Isabelle; of the duke triumphing over him and saying:

"You displeased me, hence you lost this woman; they that oppose me never get anything."

He got the type-written sheets helplessly out of the drawer and stared at them. His newspaper sense could not be beguiled. That thing was strong, convincing, a big projectile. And Dexter would never know that he had it! Again for an instant he had a half definite idea of taking the sheets to Isabelle, with an almost pathetic conviction that even she couldn't resist the actual documents, with the headlines he would write. It was a perception of the puerile absurdity of this which helped him to pull himself together a little. He was merely eddying and flopping, and anything was better than that. He turned to the proofs of articles for the morning's paper, which were always put on his desk as they accumulated whether he was there or

THE MONEY CAPTAIN

not, and he thought of staying down and making up the paper. But as soon as his mind began touching the actual details it was like flicking a sore spot. How useless those things seemed! He looked around the dingy little room as though in some of its cracks and crannies he might find a clew to that outlet of action which was absolutely necessary.

Abruptly, all became clear and simple to him. He pulled up a pad of paper and began writing in a large, plain, homely hand. After a while he got up and took off his coat and cuffs for easier action, and resumed his writing. Already he felt relieved. His anger had found a vent.

When he finished the article two hours and a half later, and revised it and wrote the headlines, he had grown quite sane. His will had emerged from the flood of passion and impotent resentment. He had kept his word to Isabelle; but he had written an article about Dexter which he believed the duke would remember. The immediate pretext was that the amendments to the Northwestern Gas ordinance would again come before the city council Monday evening, it being understood that the mayor would return them with a veto.

Leggett staid to write the headlines; and

went to his hotel finally, bitter indeed and depressed and weary, but with a clear mind.

When he read the paper in the morning, the article struck him as even more incisive, bold and challenging than he had thought it over night. It was a blow in the face, and it comforted him. The article was editorial in tone, but it occupied the most conspicuous part of the front page of the newspaper. In the center of that page appeared a big portrait of Dexter Over it was printed: "Archibald Dexter, Duke of Gas," and, beneath: "This is a good likeness of the man who systematically corrupts the city council."

The article accused Dexter specifically of bribing members of the council to vote for the amendments to the Gas ordinance. "When the amendments were passed," it said, "Dexter's hand was visible everywhere. All the steps were taken under personal direction of his creatures. The environs of the council chamber swarmed with the unclean animalcules which infest the Dexter body politic. Half an hour before the council convened, his confidential messenger hastened from the ducal palace on Drexel Boulevard, scene of so many admired social functions, to the agents who were anxiously awaiting final word from the great corruptionist in an office near the city hall."

It occurred to Leggett that he might have been somewhat less specific. If Dexter should take up the challenge—but probably he would not, because every word printed was absolutely true. For his part he had gone about as far as he could. His passion had spent itself for the moment and he drifted back in the reflux. He regretted nothing; but he was a little sick of the whole business. He was ready to call this chapter of the Dexter episode closed. He had closed it with a good hard kick, and he was well enough content although he had lost the main point he played for. There were other resources.

Entering the anteroom of his den, he was thinking of that investigation of grand jury work which he had proposed some time before. He was about to brush aside the unkempt man who got in his way. The man, however, got still more in his way and extended a folded paper. "Warrant," he said, apologetically.

As soon as Leggett understood that he had been arrested on Dexter's complaint for criminal libel he asked the constable to sit down and told the city editor to telephone for Bascom. Then he went inside and shut

THE MONEY CAPTAIN

the door—a constructive contempt which the constable took very complacently. In his own room he frowned rebelliously at the warrant. It was certainly in execrable taste on the part of Fate. He had done with the thing and here it was bobbing up senselessly to irritate him. It was crowding a man who had shown his willingness to quit. It appeared that he was unwarrantably beset from all sides. Well, he could fight if everybody insisted upon it.

When Bascom came, Leggett went with him and the officer and gave bail and Bascom set off to arrange that the hearing should be postponed a few days so that they might have time to talk over the situation.

Leggett took dinner down-town, therefore, and went to Bascom's office immediately afterwards. There was little sociability between them. Nearly all the capital stock of The Eagle Publishing Company stood in Bascom's name; but he was, in fact, as to the larger part of it merely a trustee. Leggett owned a little of the stock and he had an option running for a term of years on a majority of the shares. The real ownership lay with nearly a dozen persons who had in one way and another become creditors of the paper and its former proprietors. To them it represented a doubtful and exceed-

THE MONEY CAPTAIN

ingly troublesome debt, and the arrangement by which Leggett came in was that the stock should be put in the hands of a trustee, while he should be given complete direction of the paper for a period.

Bascom's law office was neither large nor pretentious. It comprised but three rooms in a building on La Salle Street which a young lawyer, striking for a foot-hold, would have rejected as too old-fashioned and cheap-looking. Few clients came to Bascom's office; but those that came counted. In these three rather shabby rooms a dozen large properties were managed and Bascom himself was a rich man.

The elevator was not running when Leggett arrived, and the editor climbed two flights of broad, winding stairs. The hall on the third floor was dark and the door to Bascom's office was locked and unlighted. Leggett was half minded to go away, but he folded his arms and leaned against the wall, waiting. Ten minutes, perhaps, passed, not to the improvement of Leggett's temper. Then he heard a slow, heavy step ascending the stairs, and was dimly aware of a figure coming down the hall. The editor did not move as Bascom came up to the door, fumbled for his keys, then for the lock, all the time puffing softly into his whiskers

THE MONEY CAPTAIN

from the exertion of climbing the stairs. Leggett thought of stepping up abruptly, in the gentle hope of scaring Bascom; but he waited, and only entered the room after Bascom had lit the gas. The lawyer, solid and pursy, flirted the match in his right hand to extinguish it, and peered, blinking, at the big form in the door.

"Come in, Mr. Leggett," he said; "you're right on time."

"I'm always prompt," Leggett replied calmly. He let Bascom come back and close the door, and stood aside while the lawyer took off his overcoat and hat and went to the inner room. He even let Bascom call, "Come in here, Mr. Leggett," before he offered to follow.

Bascom was washing his hands at a bowl in the corner when Leggett entered. He completed the operation, very deliberately. The carpet in this room had been worn to a threadbare whitishness. There was a desk, a couple of chairs, an old horse-hair sofa. Leggett sat on the sofa and the lawyer came over to the revolving cane-seated chair by the desk. His head was of the same solid structure and appearance as his body. He wore a full beard, neatly trimmed and streaked with gray, and a turn-down collar with a little black tie. As he sat down, swinging the chair around to face Leggett, he made a little clearing of his throat and an elevation of his thick eyebrows which struck Leggett as somehow pious and put him at once in an aggressive attitude.

"I don't like the way you're treating Mr. Dexter, Mr. Leggett," said Bascom at once, in a perfectly cool and matter of fact way.

Leggett merely waited.

"It seems to me," he went on, in his perfectly cool and matter of fact way, "that it won't do this newspaper property any good. It hasn't the approval of the substantial element that any enterprise ought to stand well with if it's going to succeed."

Leggett was surprised. Bascom had never before shown any inclination to interfere. But he merely said, calmly, "I believe questions of that sort were left to me—somebody has to decide, you know."

"Yes, that's true," Bascom replied, dryly and judicially. "The agreement under which you have charge of the paper gives you very large powers, very wide discretion. Still, I don't think that the men who really have the interest in the paper would be compelled to sit by and see the property recklessly depreciated. There is a point at which they would, in my opinion, be upheld in interfering. It seems to me that we may be approaching that point."

He spoke without a touch of feeling of any sort, almost as an automaton might be supposed to speak. His stout red hands were folded calmly over his stomach, and Leggett, looking up at him, perceived his point of view—that of the dry, firm, immobile guardian with whom the conservation of property had grown to be a sort of fireless passion.

"It's like this, Mr. Bascom," Leggett replied, reduced to the councillor's judicial and dispassionate attitude; "nothing will save a newspaper except a newspaper sense; nothing will build it up except that. You may have everything else you like, but if you haven't the newspaper sense you will never succeed. The newspaper sense is a special mental quality. I think it is just as distinct as the judicial sense or the commercial sense—almost as the art sense. It was the theory of the men who put me in control of the paper that I had it. You may have it, but I doubt it. This matter of the Dexter articles comes within my province. If I'm not competent to judge there I'm quite useless in the position I occupy."

Bascom stroked his beard thoughtfully a moment. "Well, you may be right," he

THE MONEY CAPTAIN

admitted reluctantly. "Those articles seem to be bad for the property, and two or three other parties in interest who spoke to me after this Langworthy suit was brought, thought the same way. I don't think your arrest will help the property any, and it will probably be followed by a suit for damages against the paper."

"You get my point," said Leggett, as having ended the discussion on his side. "If I'm wrong here I'm probably wrong all the way through—and I may remind you that the property has improved a good deal under my management."

"Yes, that's so," said Bascom "Well," he added, after a brief pause, "I thought it right to call your attention to this matter. So long as the property shows improvement I don't know that anything will be done." He stopped, with an implication, which Leggett found rather irritating, that if anything should be done it would be all up with the editor.

Bascom made the soft clearing of his throat and elevated his eyebrows "Of course the personal side of it is no affair of mine," he said dryly, "but Dexter is a powerful antagonist; his influence reaches everywhere. If he starts in to prosecute you in earnest—" he did not finish the sentence;

THE MONEY CAPTAIN

but he smiled; and Leggett could see the lawyer, his hands folded calmly on his stomach, his solid head a little to one side in a judicial attitude, watching the departure of one Hamilton Leggett for the penitentiary in exactly the same mind that he would watch the transit of Venus.

"Well, on the personal side, Dexter and I can fight it out," he said. "I sent for you to-day, because in a way it fell into your field—this arrest. I don't know whether you would care to continue in the case or not."

"No; I shouldn't," Bascom replied calmly. "I was going to talk with you about that. It's outside of my line of practice, and my other engagements wouldn't permit—that is as to the trial of the case in court. Of course I should like to be consulted, and if my advice is worth anything it can be used. In a way this matter affects the property, you know."

"Oh, certainly," said Leggett.

"Unless you have somebody you prefer I will call in Mr. Tollifer—a very able man, you know—and I think you need able counsel."

"Well, I dare say Tollifer will do as well as anybody. I know him pretty well," Leggett replied.

THE MONEY CAPTAIN

When Leggett left the office the appointment with Tollifer the next forenoon was far from his mind. Bascom's attitude was creating an impression as of a ponderous and immutable force that was slowly taking form and weight in opposition to him. It was not exactly what the lawyer had said about the possible interference by the stockholders, nor about the formidable character of Dexter's antagonism and the subtle ramifications of his influence; but partly these more tangible things and partly Bascom's very air as being a sort of embodiment of the dry power of wealth, of vested rights. That sense of being beset from all sides weighed upon his mind. Almost for the first time in his life he felt himself insecure and in a helpless minority. The strength of his heart centered in a slow, bitter, dogged rage. Let them all come at him. He was not going to quail.

As to this libel prosecution, if only he could use that affidavit! Ah! Isabelle had demanded that weapon of him in order to save her pretty little simpering sentiments. Well, let her keep it; let all of them take all the advantage they could get of him! Thank the Lord, her little sugar-coated sensibilities and her tiny perfumed honor to the Deeres should be saved. He had a sense of Isabelle

THE MONEY CAPTAIN

awaiting the crash with some pretty little sentiments, but without any real appreciation of what her intervention had cost him. His mind flavored all things with its pungent gall. Perhaps after the crash she and Dexter would make an interesting comparison of notes. That pig, Dexter! That, after all, he should triumph, and through this inadvertence; without any merit on his part!

The trouble was that in this stupid law business a man could do nothing; he had no chance. Everything must be left to the plodding lawyers and to the dull, owly court. It was like asking a man to be quartered and to smile and look pleasant while the operation went on. It was the dreary, musty impersonal things that he was asked to fight by proxy. It was in the manipulation of this dry machinery, after all, that Dexter's sinister power lay. If only a man could jump in and make a stroke of his own! Again that air of Bascom's, as of a typification of Property, that would sit calmly by and see him sent to the penitentiary, or hanged for that matter, came back and oppressed him.

He saw Dexter's letter in the *Clarion* in the morning as he was sitting at the breakfast table; but he did not read it because he

THE MONEY CAPTAIN

thought two or three of the guests were watching him. He read the *Index* with an air of unconcern, and even talked jocularly about the return of the base ball season. After breakfast he stopped in the lobby and bought some cigars and joked with the two men who were buying morning papers at the stand. When he got into his own room he dropped in a chair and opened the *Clarion* to that column on the second page, of which he had caught only the headlines, "Reply to the *Eagle*. Mr. Dexter writes a pointed letter regarding a valued contemporary and its editor, Hamilton J. Leggett. Declares that he will prosecute the latter to the end."

The letter was addressed to the editor of the *Clarion*, and ostensibly its text was a sneering editorial article in an afternoon paper which commented on Leggett's arrest and asked if the duke of Gas purposed reforming the press in addition to other and multifarious duties. Dexter began clumsily by saying that his attention had been called to this editorial article. "I should not think of attempting to reform the press," he wrote. "Up to this time I have been satisfied to attend to my own business and let the newspapers attend to theirs, although a number of them seem to think that includes paying a

THE MONEY CAPTAIN

good deal of attention to my affairs. Everybody who reads the newspapers knows how reckless many of them are in attacking interests and persons that happen to incur their displeasure. I have taken my share of this kind of general abuse as patiently as anybody. But it is obvious that if any man is to have any security at all for his character and reputation the line must be drawn somewhere. There ought to be a man in Chicago, or a good many of them for that matter, who would say to the newspapers, 'If you lie too villainously about me I will punish you.' The mere snapping and snarling at my heels I don't bother about; but if a newspaper brands me as a thief it must prove it or somebody must go to jail. The *Evening Call* insinuates that my arrest of Leggett was a bluff. I will prove that it is not a bluff. My purpose in writing this is partly to pledge myself to use every effort to see that Hamilton J. Leggett is sent to the penitentiary. Personally I don't care whether Leggett goes to the penitentiary or only to the bridewell; but I propose to make an example of him. Such skulking and cowardly attacks must cease. In the article on account of which I procured Leggett's arrest, that gentleman asks a good many questions as to what I did about certain

THE MONEY CAPTAIN

matters. If Leggett really wanted those questions answered why doesn't he come to me and ask me? As a newspaper man he knows that I am always accessible to representatives of the press when my engagements permit me to be. He knows that if they come and ask questions that are of public interest I always answer their questions. If Leggett really wanted to know why didn't he come to me and ask me? Why doesn't he come now? He knows where my office is and where my house is; or he can get the information from the city directory. Probably he is afraid to ask the questions to my face."

To Leggett it had the effect of a final taunt. It heightened the gall of that hateful image of Dexter standing over him, smug, insolent, relying on his millions; it gave to the image the suggestion of a sinister grin, indulged just before the knife descended on the victim, which was Leggett's self.

The interview with Tollifer did not help his equanimity. That lean, steady-eyed criminal lawyer took a serious view of the case, especially after Leggett's admission by implication that he had no specific evidence that would stand in court.

"He's a nasty antagonist, is Dexter," said

Tollifer; "his influence reaches everywhere and it's a nasty thing to fight, or to have fighting you."

Leggett came away sullenly. Before he left the office in the early evening he took out that type-written manuscript with the notarial seal. A dozen schemes for bringing it into the fight without publishing it himself occurred to his mind; but in the end he had to put all of them by. As to that he was firmly tied. Yet those four type-written pages might be his life.

Well, he could give up his life—Dexter could have his way—ah, Dexter! It would be Dexter's triumph. He could see the duke standing over him, secure in his money, wrapt in his insolent thievery as in armor, having all that indefinite yet ponderous and insuperable weight of Property which Bascom represented on his side.

Something in him that would not contemplate defeat, that cried out to stand before this Dexter and measure itself against him and show him it was master, stirred mightily. A torrent of wrath suffused his mind. He went rapidly from the office, plunged across the street and summoned a hack, into which he climbed with an effect of projecting himself recklessly. As the carriage rolled over the rough paving all restraints fell swiftly from his mind and even amid his passion he felt almost serene. At least he was being himself—and Dexter had explicitly invited it.

CHAPTER XV

This sentence in Leggett's article, "Half an hour before the council convened his trusted messenger hastened from the ducal palace on Drexel Boulevard, scene of so many admired social functions, to the agents who were anxiously awaiting final word from the great corruptionist in an office near the city hall," leapt from the type and expanded before Nidstrom's eyes with the significance of a conspicuous, accusing forefinger.

The unclean suggestion of that errand to Deere's office had been distasteful and annoying to him. But it had been one of those private things that one may temporize with, like the little lie that nobody can detect, the little meanness done secretly. Now it was dragged into the middle of the street and advertised with big placards. When he went down to the Gas office he half supposed that the duke might demand an explanation as to how Leggett came to know of his errand. As to that he felt a certain hardihood and a clear conscience.

THE MONEY CAPTAIN

He went over the facts. Of course he should tell the truth if it were demanded on the other side; and in spite of his disgust and resentment he could not help a loyalty to Dexter which made even an enforced aid to the opposition seem some way cowardly and ingrateful. However, word came down that Dexter would not be at the office, and he did not come next day. Nidstrom read of his appearing in the justice's court when Leggett's hearing was continued, and he read his letter to the *Clarion* next morning.

The secretary looked back with a new and unexpected regret at the loss of his Gas money. With that in his pocket he might turn in earnest toward the consideration of that offer to take over the abstract-of-title business in High Grove, respecting which he had gone into some furtive correspondence. The air of the Gas office suffocated him.

It was after five o'clock Tuesday when he got the telephone message summoning him to Dexter's house after dinner, and by that time he felt a certain indifferent hardihood as to whatever Dexter might do or say. He was sick of Dexter and of the world in which Dexter lived.

Walking over to Drexel Boulevard, he

THE MONEY CAPTAIN

told himself that after all Dexter was only a shadow, merely a passing, personified figment of the vast stirrings of industry and accumulation of wealth that came out of the new country's rich soil, as though all the wheat and corn could be heaped into a huge mound for a moment after harvest, before it flowed away in the thousand channels of demand.

That idea was strongly in his mind as he went up to the carved oak doors; yet, in spite of that the scene within instantly imposed upon his imagination as though the display of wealth in that baronial hall defied him to deny its reality and solidity. In spite of himself, he could not meet the challenge. Treading again those broad stairs, the air of spaciousness and richness conquered him. It even entertained him as he ascended to travel in so short a way along that gold and crimson path which the magnificent make through history. He fancied, that it was not so very different from going in to Sardanapalus. The brass electrolier, that idle, curiously wrought elevator cage down there—they were real.

He found Dexter at the table lighted by the shaded lamp in the room he knew. The duke had his inevitable effect of being absorbed in the great, intricate coil of business which he seemed to spin continually. He glanced up and nodded hospitably, and motioned to a seat.

"I won't be at the office to-morrow, Mr. Nidstrom," he said, and he began explaining a statement which he wished prepared and forwarded to him at a New York hotel.

While the two were thus engaged, Nidstrom tilting his chair forward and making memoranda on a pad of paper at the corner of the table, as Dexter explained, the footman entered, with his usual air of glancing at a lowly world over his collar, bearing a card. Nidstrom noticed that he carried the card in his hand, which appeared to the secretary, from his acquaintance with stage footmen, as a contretemps, and when the servant walked straight up to the duke and held out the card, it was as though Dexter, too, was of that lowly world from which the footman was walled by his collar.

Evidently, however, neither of these suggestions was apparent to Dexter; or, if it was, he did not mind it. He took the card, glanced at it, and held it impassively in his hand a moment. Then he shifted his attitude in the chair slightly, and twisted a bunch of his beard, thoughtfully, all the time regarding the card which he held in his hand.

THE MONEY CAPTAIN

When he spoke he addressed Nidstrom, but without looking at him. His face relaxed a very little, as though he were moved by an amusing thought, but otherwise his manner was quite grave. The footman waited, impersonally.

"I wish you'd step in the next room a minute, Mr. Nidstrom," he said. "It won't be long. Find Mr. Nidstrom a seat in there," he added, to the footman.

The footman stepped aside, as to conduct Nidstrom, and the secretary, a little puzzled, secretly a little offended, got up without replying.

The servant crossed the room to a small solid door near the further corner. He opened this door and entered before Nidstrom. As he did so Dexter's voice called, sharply, "Henry!"

The footman turned abruptly and brushed against Nidstrom, who was in the doorway, and went back to the table, leaving the secretary standing at the threshold of a dark room which appeared to be a sleeping apartment. He wondered if the servant were not really ill-mannered; but perhaps the stage servants were wrong.

When the footman returned, which was within the space of a minute, he got a chair from the shadows of the room and placed it

THE MONEY CAPTAIN

back a couple of yards from the door. Nidstrom sat down. Going out the footman turned, at the door, and said in a low and soft and insinuating voice, "Mr. Dexter may call you in." Then he disappeared, first drawing the door about two-thirds shut. An instant after he disappeared there was a strong flooding of light in the other room, and Nidstrom perceived that all the electric lamps had been turned on.

Sitting in the chair that had been placed for him, his vision comprehended a broadening strip across the rear of the other room. The back of Dexter's chair and about half of Dexter's figure were visible. The shadows fell so that Nidstrom himself was in darkness.

Perceiving this arrangement in the first surprised, doubtful outward glance, Nidstrom revolted. A sweep of indignation moved him. Plainly, he was posited as a spy and eavesdropper. He thought of walking out, at least of closing the door—but then, it might be innocent enough. He fancied Dexter glancing up at his protest, impassive, a little contemptuous, and with that imagining his scruples appeared tiny and insignificant. At least, he could wait.

He settled back in the chair and tried to forget his environment; but in spite of himself his straining ears caught a faint sound from the silently swinging door and the noiseless carpet of the other room. He knew that somebody had been ushered in, and it was like the lifting of the curtain on the play.

For a moment there was dead silence, and Nidstrom fancied the withdrawal of the footman, leaving the outer door ajar, since he could not hear it close.

After an instant that stretched out long and ominous to the waiting secretary, Dexter's voice sounded, very calmly; but with a sound that touched all of Nidstrom's nerves to a higher tension, as though it were the beginning of the denouement to which he was privy.

"You wished to see me?" the duke said.

"You invited me, I believe," said another voice, and Nidstrom's lips parted, his heart beat faster.

It was Leggett.

In a flash Nidstrom saw the two men confronting each other, full of hate, Dexter sitting at the table, outwardly impassive, but touched with contempt; Leggett standing in the center of the room, his thumbs hooked in his overcoat pockets, his hat in one hand, looking down at his enemy.

It was the first time that either had looked

THE MONEY CAPTAIN

the other squarely in the face, and at the sight each felt his contempt grow larger and hotter. Dexter was the last man to take an added value to himself from those rich surroundings; but against the sumptuous background of his study the contrast of this figure from nowhere, its thumbs hooked in its overcoat pockets, with a slight suggestion of swagger, a hard little dent in its smooth chin, a mop of sandy hair over its brow, and its belligerent little tuft standing up humorously in the center of its crown, suggested something cheekily mendicant, something blossomed from the purlieus.

Leggett looked down at the broad, pudgy figure by the table, thick-necked, ruddy, low-browed, bristling with coarse black hair, and he thought: "So this is the sacred pig to which I am to be fed." He felt a touch of something like relief. This fellow was not one of whom he could possibly be afraid. All this was in a second. When Dexter spoke, his voice showed repression.

"I did not invite you," he said, "but you see, I don't avoid you. What do you want?"

It was not practicable to say, "I want to ease my soul of your imputation of personal cowardice; I want to demonstrate to my fill that I'm not afraid of you anywhere; I want to look into your eye and make you feel that you can't frighten me; I want to dash myself against the bar that has got in my way. Incidentally, perhaps, I want to insult you to your face as well as in print."

It was not easy to say this.

Instead, Leggett said, in an even voice: "Did you bribe some members of the city council to amend the Northwestern Gas ordinance?"

Dexter compressed his lips, and his hand moved in the direction of the button at the corner of the desk. He had not taken the measure of the man. He had supposed it was going to be some kind of complaint, some kind of suggestion of compromise.

"You will have to prove that I did," he replied shortly.

"Did you employ Richard Deere, an attorney, as your go-between, and did he employ ex-Alderman Simpson, and did you——"

"Why do you stand there repeating those parrot questions?" Dexter cut in harshly and stridently. "You know they are all lies. What did you come here for?"

"To ask a few questions, as you publicly invited me to," said Leggett, woodenly. "Did you send a messenger to Deere——"

"Your questions are impertinent. You know those suggestions are all lies," said

Dexter, with a touch more of excitement. "If you have anything decent to ask me, ask it. If you haven't, get out, or I'll call a servant and have you thrown out."

Leggett moved a mere foot's length nearer to the table, and went on without changing his tone, but more rapidly. "So it's to be a question of servants and hired thugs and hired henchmen of all kinds, and not of just you and me, is it? That was all a poor bluff—your letter to the *Clarion*. You wouldn't think for a minute of coming out of your deep rat-hole, with all sorts of hired creatures and traps and made-up pitfalls to protect you, and looking me in the eye—just you and me alone—and telling me you proposed to send me to the penitentiary?" He took another brief step toward the desk, and lifted his right hand, with the felt hat in it, and pointed that article as in derision at the figure by the table. "That's why I object to you, Dexter. That's why I can't help roasting you, you know. You're a bold man, with all your barricades and traps and hired men around you; but to come out into the open, just yourself alone, and answer a challenge—Huh!" He made a sound through his nostrils.

Both Dexter's hands lay, palm down,

upon the desk; he was bending forward slightly, his blazing eyes fixed on the insolent figure in the center of the room, and his speech seemed to have been cut off.

"That's why I don't like you, Dexter; you're really only a fat rat," Leggett added.

"Oh, as to that," Dexter cried thickly—speech still seemed difficult; but he got up and started around the end of the table.

There was no piece or part in Dexter's mind for cowardice to lay hold of; and no man relied less upon his accessories. Deep in him his reply to Leggett's challenge was the reply of the bull. His contempt for the editor was complete. There was no mistaking the purport of the look that blazed out of his eyes.

Leggett saw him coming, his head settled down on his thick neck, and restrained the grin which would have been the fit expression of his ferocious joy.

Neither man thought whether the other was armed. Perhaps it would have made no difference to either. The situation in a way was the reduction of the two characters to their final quotients. For, after all, these invented accessories of ink and type and lawyers and financial machinations were but poor devices for their impatience. To

THE MONEY CAPTAIN

plunge through them and lay a manual hold with the naked hand—that was much more satisfactory.

Nidstrom was standing in the doorway to the bedroom, horrified, ready to cry out, ready to rush between them, ready to forbid the murderous clash——

And then a quick, high-keyed yip and bark rent the electrified air; an elongated woolly ball appeared, from nowhere, on the carpet by Leggett's heels, darting back and forth, barking and snapping at the bottom of his trousers' leg.

Almost before this abrupt new note became incorporated in the tragic atmosphere the outer door to the study, already slightly ajar, was pushed further open, and Miss Lilian West, blooming, smiling, charmingly dressed, appeared on the threshold with a quick little "Oh!" of apology at sight of Leggett.

Holding the knob of the door, the girl bent forward gracefully, snapping her white fingers and calling, "Major! Major!" and screwing her pretty lips together to make a sound at the dog as of exaggerated kissing.

But the dog, backing a little away from Leggett, eyed the trousers' leg with head cockishly to one side, and ignored the summons.

THE MONEY CAPTAIN

The girl showed her white teeth in a brilliant smile which included both her uncle's downcast face and Leggett's impassive back. She colored slightly also as she came quickly over the carpet, stooped and gathered the dog in her arms. When she straightened up she was at Leggett's side and a little further advanced in the room than he was, so that she looked into his face. At that moment his face was quite composed and blank. It would have done very well for a butler.

Miss West did not speak, but without seeming to stop in her movements, she managed to make a tiny pause. She was quite willing that her uncle should indulge her passion for trying all sorts of people by introducing her to this robust young stranger. But Dexter's eyes were fixed on the carpet. He never raised them.

The girl went out, without haste, carrying her dog, and Nidstrom dropped back into the shadows of the bedroom. He realized that this little haphazard interpolation of burlesque had spoiled the tragedy.

The two men realized it also. The intrusion instantly swung them back into a definite relationship with their environment. It brought in the neighbors, so that each of them became aware that a duke and an

THE MONEY CAPTAIN

editor wrestling around over a study floor constituted a picture that was not in keeping with the rest of the decorations.

Naturally, the reminder bore more strongly upon Dexter than upon Leggett. He rested his hand on the corner of the desk.

"I suppose there's nothing further," he said, drily. He gave one quick upward glance and Leggett saw that the underlids of his eyes were slightly inflamed, giving those organs a haggard appearance.

Leggett hesitated an instant. He was quite aware, without the duke's saying so, that there was nothing further; that the fine naked moment of a possible homicide had definitely passed, and that anything more would be simply boorish and blackguardly. All the same, he felt somewhat encouraged because of those inflamed eyes.

"Good night," he said, ironically, and went out.

Nidstrom waited for the duke's summons in revolt and disgust.

Several minutes passed, it seemed to him, and he got up abruptly and entered the other room. He was not hired to spend his time lurking in somebody's bedroom.

Dexter sat at the table, his hands on the arms of his chair. It struck Nidstrom at once that he was suffering, and the secretary hastened forward, with contrition for his rebellion.

"You feel upset," he began hurriedly——

"No," said Dexter, tersely, even harshly. In a moment he pulled himself up to the table and reached for the bundle of papers that had been in his hands when Leggett's card came in.

"Sit down, Mr. Nidstrom," he said, and this time his voice was smooth and courteous, as Nidstrom knew it habitually in the Gas office. "Now, these comparisons," he began, taking up the business where it had been broken off.

Nidstrom noticed that in handling the papers his hand shook a little, and that he paused rather long between sentences sometimes; but this was only for a few moments, and he was soon going serenely ahead with his effect of being a powerful, tireless, perfectly adjusted machine that ground at a set rate day in and day out.

It required, perhaps, half an hour to go over the affair. When it was finished, as it seemed to Nidstrom, Dexter turned over a sheet of paper and looked at it as though he had a cursory interest in it, and as he was thus employed, he asked:

"What do you hear of Drouillard?"

"Oh, I haven't heard much except what

has been in the papers,"Nidstrom answered, shaping his notes to put them in his pocket. He owned to a little surprise at this personal question.

Dexter leaned back in his chair, and looked over at him and smiled a little. It was a very frank smile so far as it went, and Nidstrom recognized it as a sign of one of those rare times when the duke proposed to be sociable for a moment.

"So far as I have been able to find out he made a very complete bust of it," he added, smiling himself in recognition of the joke of losing one's money through having intrusted it to a fellow like Drouillard.

"Yes, I guess he did," said Dexter. He mused a moment. "Do you know this newspaper fellow?" he asked abruptly, his face quite composed.

"Leggett? Yes, I know him," Nidstrom replied, as though his surprise had touched a spring that released the speech.

"What does he want?" Dexter asked.

Nidstrom pondered it a moment. "I fancy he doesn't know," he replied, smiling a little. "What does any man want after the scrimmage has begun—when he's fighting and his blood is hot?"

"Why, I never did that man a cent's worth of injury in my life until he began black-

THE MONEY CAPTAIN

guarding me and my family," Dexter answered, with a note of surprise. "It was all his doing."

"Probably not," said Nidstrom; "but you kept on doing the things he said you mustn't do. He has persuaded himself that you're a public enemy, therefore his enemy."

Dexter looked wonderingly at his secretary a moment; then an abrupt, explosive, contemptuous puff of laughter burst through his bearded lips. "Good Lord!" he exclaimed, as though it were too absurd for further consideration. "Why, I have my work to do, haven't I? What would become of this Gas company if I stopped to study the crotchets of every impractical addle-pate that bobs up? What did Leggett ever do? What did the rest of these hand-made prophets ever do? If they don't like the way I run this Gas concern, let them build up another one and see how much better they can do with it."

"The critics always say that's no argument," Nidstrom replied, smiling, but stubborn—partly because of that wait in the bedroom.

"Well, I'm going to send that fellow to the penitentiary," said Dexter coolly, but as ending the matter, and he straightened up to the table.

THE MONEY CAPTAIN

"Will it be worth while?" Nidstrom suggested, boldly.

"I think so," Dexter replied abruptly, not in a way to encourage further suggestions.

Nevertheless, Nidstrom, rising, said: "Wouldn't it be more satisfactory if he would stop the fighting?"

Dexter glanced up. The underlids of his eyes were still inflamed. He paused an instant, then said, "I'd like to see some signs of repentance on his part before I said as to that."

Nidstrom hung, reluctantly, in the act of going for a second. "Well, I'll get up these statements to-morrow," he said.

The word seemed to please Dexter. "Yes—I'm obliged to you for coming over," he said.

The unusual acknowledgment softened Nidstrom's heart somewhat. "Oh, not at all. Good night," he said.

Dexter's cool, even voice, the compelling but not unkindly voice of the Gas office, called after him, "Good night"; and as Nidstrom went out of the door, he had a last glimpse of the duke sitting at the table serenely immersed in work.

CHAPTER XVI

Outside, the night air had a touch of spring, and Nidstrom felt a homesick love of it as he walked slowly down from the granite porch. On the cement walk he paused, looking back. Even under that vast and luminously dim void of the night the great house made its bold and solid effect. He could not make a valid denial of the verity which that house asserted, and his helplessness to deny it troubled him. The fortress-like porch seemed to claim an inscrutable kinship with Roman palaces. High up in the broad façade a half-drawn curtain gave a glimpse that teasingly suggested romance.

Against Nidstrom's revolt at his innocent complicity in the Deere episode, against the menial eavesdropping, the motive of loyalty weighed. Nidstrom was pursued by the conception of a certain faithful relationship to an historic figure. His duke insisted upon being real. Merely to imagine himself saying to Dexter, "I object to the moral plane of your enterprise; my conscience dictates that I leave your service;" to call up Dexter's figure and imagine himself saying that was to think of the impossible. Dexter's presence, even imagined, made it impossible. It would be like saying to a competent commander on a battle-field, "If you swear, I cannot follow you." Nidstrom realized all this tangibly, and tried to find the reasons of it as he walked slowly west.

The gas lamps burned broad and still in the calm air, and his shadow fell, now shortening before him, now lengthening behind him, and now wavering through an irregular arc at his side as he passed one lamp after another. Somewhere on every long stretch of street which he intersected in his eastward walk there was a flock of bicyclers with twinkling lights like large fireflies, and tinkling bells, their voices calling gayly into the mellow dark. Even the cable trains on Cottage Grove Avenue, where the riders showed a preference for the open seats of the grip-cars and the windows of the other cars were pushed down to let the air circulate, took on unwontedly a festal suggestion. Only the interminable rows of houses seemed joyless and dreary.

Nidstrom crossed Tremont Avenue as he had the other streets, and stopped only at the stone wall that fenced the railroad tracks on the lake shore. The edge of the water

THE MONEY CAPTAIN

whispered in the dark, and further out the great softly moving expanse was darkly luminous under the light of the stars. It suggested to him again that deep heart of peace and beauty which the environment at the country-place had suggested, to which it seemed one could escape so easily. The huge, pent, grimy, breathless, grasping camp at his back seemed ineffably dreary and futile—just the dark place for a Dexter to pile up a vast ducal estate of riches, all pillage and spoils. He tried to remove himself in fancy from the city's environment, to look at Dexter across an interval of verdure, through a medium of fresh air, and it then seemed to him that he could consider the duke philosophically, that he could rid his will of that fealty which Dexter's presence imposed upon him. The problem was this: How could a man feel bound to a cause at which his conscience revolted—still bound when the bonds hurt his self-respect? He could condemn Dexter endlessly; but as soon as he imagined himself in Dexter's presence he could not help an admiration and a loyalty. The detestable aspect of that errand to Deere's startled his conscience. Leggett was under accusation. He might be sent to the penitentiary for criminal libel. Of course, the mere going from

THE MONEY CAPTAIN

Dexter to Deere that night was conclusive of nothing; but in an affair of that kind it might easily turn the scale in Leggett's favor. Yet to imagine himself standing out before Dexter and testifying to that had the effect of a low treachery. Was he simply afraid of Dexter?

Coming back to the house in Tremont Avenue, he went up the steps and entered slowly. Arthur and Nell were in the library, and he stepped in and sat on the edge of a chair without taking off his hat, and with an effect of not definitely joining them.

The effect was so patent that Arthur said, "Have you registered? If you have no baggage you must pay in advance."

Nidstrom smiled patiently, and removed his hat. "I thought I might go out again," he said, apologetically, and looking at Nell.

"Why, it's rather late," she said, provisionally, and not quite certain, in respect of the invitation in his eye, as to how serious it was.

"Yes, and if you go the youngster will be sure to wake up and howl for his mother," Arthur put in. "I think the moon has got on Victor's brain."

"Would you like to go for a walk?" Nell asked quickly.

THE MONEY CAPTAIN

"Oh, no; it's late," Nidstrom answered definitely, and tossed his hat to a chair. After all, why not there as well as any other place. "It's a perfect night, though," he added, with a momentary regret.

"And only man is vile," Arthur laughed.

Nell came gravely over to the stool beside his chair and sat down.

"I feel rather sick of it all," said Nidstrom, soberly, and again his eye sought his wife. "Leggett came over there to Dexter's to-night, and the duke put me in a bedroom where I'd be handy to overhear and to interfere. It wasn't prearranged, you know. Leggett came of his own motion, looking for trouble." He told briefly the episode of the dog. "Those two men want to murder each other really. I don't know which is the worst or the most unscrupulous. It's just the successful scramble for money on one side, and the popular rage and clamor against it on the other. To talk of morals in respect of either side is like talking of decorum in respect of naked savages. Part of what Leggett says against Dexter is true. I took a message from Dexter to Deere that night the council met. But how could I go over to Leggett with that information and testimony without joining his mere selfish fight against Dexter?"

"I don't think you ought to go," said Nell quickly. "It was simply Mr. Dexter's business that he employs you for."

"But I'm responsible, am I not, just the same?" said Nidstrom.

Nell looked down thoughtfully, and would not give him the word he wished.

"Oh, well, incidents of that kind can't be helped," said Arthur, comfortingly. "They're part of the condition. It's like ducking out of the way of a cable train. You can't do it in a dignified way, and nobody thinks of it."

"One who cares for dignity might go where there are no cable trains, though," Nidstrom suggested vaguely, not looking at Nell, but hoping she would speak.

In her silence he felt again that still, uncontentious opposition to his dream, and he felt again that he stood accused, though charitably and lovingly, of an impracticable freak, a ruinous folly. He said nothing more. Presently, Arthur began talking irrepressibly about something else, and Nell got a book, and the subject stood away from them, although as to himself and Nell it was easily within beck.

Up-stairs in their own room she came over to him abruptly, after they had spoken desultorily about something else.

"Do you think it would be better up there at High Grove?" she asked, with sweetness. Her tone and manner implied a further leaning toward his wish than she had ever shown before.

He sat down, his collar half unfastened, and began very gravely, as though she had proposed that they move. "It would have been rather simple if I hadn't lost the Gas money," he said, a little doubtfully. "I mean I could have bought the abstract books then and started in clear. I've had the thing looked up pretty well—that wouldn't do any harm anyway. Of course, I should want to go up there a week and look things over before I did anything," he added, with a saving effect of conservatism. "What is the most that a man like me hopes to get here? A little peace, a little security, a little margin to his life for his friends and family, and for some books. And in the country you can get all those things at once, instead of possibly at the end of a lifetime of hard work. Here I can only be a piece in somebody's huge, grinding, soulless machine—you know that, Nell."

Nell's eyes never left him as he spoke. She slipped her arm over his shoulder. "Well, we can look it over, dear," she said, with cheerfulness. "You know it doesn't

THE MONEY CAPTAIN

make any difference to Tots and me where we are. You must do as you think best."

"But you don't think I'd like it there?" Nidstrom asked.

Nell smiled outright. "No, I don't," she said. "But I may be mistaken," she added gravely. "Seems to me that business is about the same everywhere, and you might find it dull and gossipy in a country town. I've been in the country more than you have. Suppose we say that we'll see."

"Yes, we'll see," Nidstrom added, unsatisfied.

"Of course, you know that Tots and I are ready whenever you think it best," she added, gravely.

Long after he should have been asleep, Nidstrom wrestled his problem up and down those treacherous avenues of wakeful thought that have some of the exaggerating, distorting atmosphere of dreams. At best, he could not deny that the country venture was a hazard of which Nell and Tots rather than himself were the potential victims. It seemed to him that if he could make a truce between Dexter and Leggett the acute difficulty of the situation would be removed. It appeared not at all an impossible accomplishment, and he fell asleep finally in an uncertain glow of having made the reconciliation.

CHAPTER XVII

Going to see Leggett, however, as a missionary, touching the matter of his quarrel with Dexter, was a proposition that looked quite different when he got it out in the sunlit street next morning. Not quite awake, or in his own house and room, with Nell's soft, serious black eyes looking into his eyes, it was easy to invest himself with enough ministerial character to warrant him in going to an acquaintance and saying to this effect: "Brother, you are doing wrong." But out in the sunshine, going to the railroad station and climbing into the cars with some hundreds of other men, he recognized the impossibility of taking Nell's atmosphere along with him; and he saw an atmosphereless, awkward, partly bald man coming, with embarrassment, into an editor's office, hat in hand, and saying, "Pardon me; but I came in to touch up your morals."

Toward noon he plucked up courage to telephone to Leggett and make an appointment. Half an hour later, hastening from the sandwich and tea, bolted at a lunch counter, he went up the worn stone steps, through the dingy counting room and the tunnel-like passage to the elevator, and was lifted, slowly and with ominous creakings, to the top floor.

Leggett at once took from the call the neighborly appearance which Nidstrom had thought of contriving at the opening, for as soon as he was inside the editorial den, the editor shut the door with a crash. Thus, at the expiration of half a minute, after the brief verbal feints of "How d' do?" Nidstrom found himself sitting at the end of the ancient table looking over at Leggett, who waited in polite immobility.

The editor was in better mood. Perhaps the mere impossible bravado of the visit to Dexter had cheered him. At any rate, it had given him an agreeable sense of his own hardihood, as a weapon which at the last and the worst could not be taken from him. Tollifer had dropped in, and they had gone over some points, technical and other, on which a defensive fight could be made. More than all else, Leggett felt himself in hand, shrewdly and sanely considering his position and the means of strengthening it. The result was a satisfying conviction that he was still worth several dead men.

"This libel matter between you and Dexter worries me a good deal," Nidstrom began, in a troubled way.

Leggett smiled a little.

"Why should it?" he asked, with an air of merely cursory interest. But he was very alert.

"Why—you might be right," Nidstrom explained; "you might be right—and yet——"

"And yet be unable to prove it?" Leggett suggested, with an effect of helping him out.

"Well—yes," Nidstrom admitted.

"There's a good deal in that," said Leggett. "Still, it's better to be right than be president, you know." He wondered what all this meant.

The editor's jocularity grated on the secretary's nerves. "But weren't you wrong in being right without being able to prove it?" he suggested.

"That's a matter of personal preference," Leggett replied; then, abruptly, "What is it, Mr. Nidstrom?" He wondered if the duke had sent a proposition for peace, or was merely seeking a new advantage.

"Just what I've told you," Nidstrom replied, quickly. "It seems to me useless and wanton and melancholy—this fight. You can prove nothing. Very likely Dexter will be able to punish you; and finally what will be the good of it? It will only make you and your friends more bitter and determined. I talked with Mr. Dexter about it. Of course, you understand that all I am doing now is of my own motion—talking to you just as I talked with him, because it seemed to me deplorable and melancholy and abominable."

Leggett took the liberty of not quite believing all this, but he merely asked: "That he should have me punished for criminal libel?"

"Well, yes, and that you should give him cause."

"But if I did libel him I ought to be punished, oughtn't I?"

"Oh—well, we know what the law provides," Nidstrom replied, a little uncertainly.

"Then you don't think I did libel him—as to the main charge?" After all, could the secretary be acting independently?

"I have no ground on which to form an opinion—at least not a complete opinion." Nidstrom felt that the editor had suddenly taken the interview out of his hands and was pushing him into a corner with it.

"Did you give Dexter your incomplete opinion?"

"You know our relations," said Nidstrom, impatiently.

THE MONEY CAPTAIN

Leggett passed his hand rapidly over his sandy hair, looking at the troubled man before him, and considering a number of things swiftly. Possibly, after all, Nidstrom was quite sincere. No doubt this confidential man knew something that would strengthen his defense against Dexter; something that, naturally, the secretary might not tell him nor give into his hands— unless, indeed, he presented one of those abnormal cases of a conscience developed above a consideration for material things, of which the books told. Perhaps it was worth while to try for the conscience.

"Read that," said the editor, abruptly; and he took the typewritten sheets from the drawer in his table and flung them at Nidstrom.

It was the affidavit of the alderman. When Nidstrom finished reading it, he laid it down, and his eyes remained downcast for a moment.

"Well," he said, with a sigh, "that strengthens your case, of course."

"It strengthens it with me," Leggett replied, and took up the typewritten sheets and glanced over them, as though he liked the mere marked paper. Indeed, it seemed very likely that Nidstrom was the singular man with an uncontrollable conscience.

THE MONEY CAPTAIN

The secretary looked up inquiringly.

"I haven't seen my way to use this publicly," Leggett added, calmly, "because of Deere's family—and a friend of theirs. Probably I shall not use it publicly at all; but, as you say, it strengthens my case."

"But if you can't use it——" Nidstrom objected, wonderingly.

"It convinces me, doesn't it?" Leggett replied. "I know I'm right, don't I? Suppose I can't use this. Can Dexter muzzle me, shut me up, bluff me out, send me home like a dog that's been kicked? If he's had me arrested for criminal libel on what I've published so far, he'll have me arrested for arson and bigamy before I'm done with him. Am I going to lie down and let him walk over me just because other people do?"

Leggett put these questions rapidly, looking Nidstrom in the eye, as though he were propounding a case which any reasoning man would have no trouble in deciding. He had resolved on a bold play.

"In the end he will crush you!" Nidstrom declared.

"Let him," said Leggett. "I'm not going to be crushed to-day or to-morrow. And while I hold together he won't be having a pleasant time."

Nidstrom threw up his hand. "You're

wrong, Leggett, wrong," he declared. "You think Dexter knows that he's wrong, and he thinks you know that you're wrong, and each thinks the other won't give up for mere stubbornness and deviltry. I tell you, Dexter thinks he's right just as much as you do. He'd say, what in effect you say, that unless he makes a stand against your newspapers there'll be no living with you. That it's better to be beaten in a cause like this than not to make the fight. He's as sincere as you are!"

He spoke earnestly, even with a certain excitement, because he felt deeply that he was at the nub of the difficulty.

Leggett sat in his chair looking coolly up at him, and when the sound of the secretary's voice had fully ceased in the little room, the editor said, calmly, "Ah, well, in that case it will be a beautiful fight." He believed that in the end Nidstrom would give way. It was worth trying for.

"Fight!" Nidstrom repeated, at a loss.

Leggett got up suddenly. "Why, if he thinks he's right as much as I think I'm right, we'll fight forever! When a man knows clear down to his boots that he's right, who wouldn't fight?"

Nidstrom looked up at the editor an instant.

THE MONEY CAPTAIN

"Well, I'm sorry," he said, with mournful impotence.

"Nothing to be sorry about," said Leggett, cheerfully.

Nidstrom went out feeling that the conflict was irreconcilable and ruthless; he had a vivid and sickening prevision of himself, endlessly dragged around and around in its swirls and eddies. It came back to him again and again in the afternoon. My God! Why must a man give himself over to these mad bulls?

Later than usual he sat in his den at the Gas office with the neatly folded sheets of Dexter's statement and an envelope addressed to Dexter in New York lying on the desk before him, and he felt himself before a darkened door.

Slowly and mechanically, he drew a pad of letter paper before him and began writing, with deliberation. It was nearly half an hour later that he finished the letter. It read:

"Dear Mr. Dexter:—I should give you the earliest notice possible that I have decided to leave Chicago and close with an offer to go into business in the country. This, of course, involves my resignation here. I have made the arrangement so that the date of my leaving is of no particular importance—that is, you can consult your

THE MONEY CAPTAIN

own convenience as to the time of choosing my successor. I wish to take this step in such a way as will not disturb your plans, as I am under many obligations to you for just and considerate treatment; but I write you at once rather than wait for your return, as I wish you to know of my determination as soon as possible."

He admitted, as he read it over for the third or fourth time, and took in its equivocal and apologetical effect, that it was as little like anything heroic as it could well be; but it accomplished the purpose. Finally, he folded it up, with an air of decision, inclosed it with the statement, sealed the envelope and put it in his pocket.

When he had dropped it in the letter box in the rotunda, he experienced a momentary feeling of relief. At least, the thing was irrevocably done. He was under no illusion as to the manner in which it had been accomplished. At best he had merely sneaked out, escaped with a whole skin and left his participation in the wrong to work out its evil unimpeded.

He tried to make the sacrifice of his position, his home, his environment, appear in the light of an atonement; but he did not succeed very well. He had to confess that to sacrifice his position and environment partly pleased him on its own account, and the whole affair had, in spite of him, much the look of a merely selfish step toward the fulfillment of his dream of country life.

He supposed that it must appear that way to Nell in the imperfect account that he could give her, and when he told her abruptly that he had resigned from the Gas office, and she stood silently before him, looking thoughtfully at the floor in an habitual attitude which yielded nothing but made no contention, he felt sure that she condemned him.

"I couldn't do anything else, Nellie," he said, a puckering at the corners of his eyes.

"But Mr. Dexter isn't here," she said, as with a grasp at hope.

"I wrote to him in New York. It's in the mails now. I had to do it."

Nell looked down again, and was silent for a moment. When she finally looked up her face was quite serene. "Well, it doesn't make any difference to Tots and me," she said.

CHAPTER XVIII

Nidstrom had sent off his resignation under the spurring of an intolerable situation. In the final moment of action it had been a half dogged and half desperate leap to escape; and it was only as he was on his way to the Gas office in the morning that the more intimate and detailed aspects of the case came clearly to his mind. When he entered the square and bare ante-room, it presented a subtly changed face to him, as though he had already become a stranger. He noticed the pile of letter-copying books by the press in the corner, and he remembered, with a little shock, that a month or more before he had purposed having them more systematically arranged and filed in a vault. Now he really had no right to touch them, and all the threads of those close business occupations which had been running through his brain for so many years suddenly snapped off and left him untagged, undesignated, unaddressed, unattached. For the first time he realized sharply the little death of being shaken loose from the

THE MONEY CAPTAIN

frame into which his habits had grown as a vine grows on a trellis.

It was from the stagnant oppression of this sense of being uprooted that he was aroused toward 10 o'clock by the appearance at the door of the tall office boy, who held the door open, murmuring with his habitual effect of diffidence, "A lady, Mr. Nidstrom."

Isabelle Wilder came in, with the unmistakable air of a woman bent on business.

Nidstrom hastened with some awkwardness and confusion to get her a chair, and he would have liked to thank her humbly for the brilliance of her eyes and the color in her cheek, both alluringly enhanced by her light, white veil.

Of course, he only said: "I'm glad you came to see me, even if your meter isn't running right;" but he said it with a certain relief, and he sat down, smiling and waiting.

"I suppose I shouldn't have come," she began, with hesitation; then, suddenly, earnestly, with an effect of throwing herself on his mercy, "but I must know something about it—this quarrel between Mr. Leggett and Mr. Dexter."

Nidstrom smiled a little at her earnestness. "Why," he said, deliberately, "I suppose the main facts have been pretty well aired by this time."

THE MONEY CAPTAIN

"Yes—but will Mr. Dexter try to—to——" She found the word very difficult.

"Convict him?" Nidstrom suggested softly.

"Yes, I am quite sure that he will try to."

Isabelle caught eagerly at the possible inference. "But he can't?" she asked, quickly.

Nidstrom smiled a little again, very indulgently, and the woman, for all her concern, felt no offense in it. "Well, that is uncertain," he said. "I don't know that Leggett himself feels at all sure as to that. I talked with him yesterday." It was in his mind to show her that his sympathies were at least not arrayed against the editor.

"And he felt uncertain?" she asked, with a kind of despair.

"I don't mean that he felt dubious—no, not uncertain," Nidstrom corrected. "He felt ready. He did not know, and nobody knows, how the thing will come out. Leggett looks the situation squarely in the face. He doesn't deceive himself, and he is ready for whatever may come." He spoke more firmly, even with a touch of resolution. Whatever were exactly his own ideas in respect of Leggett's standing; he was quite willing and a little more than willing to magnify him to this pretty, eager woman who was so evidently in love with him.

THE MONEY CAPTAIN

Isabelle looked at him with a grave, half questioning helplessness for a moment. Then she said, abruptly: "What do you think, Mr. Nidstrom?"

Nidstrom deliberated a moment. If he had been accused he would not have denied that he liked the flattering appeal of those bright eyes; perhaps he would not have denied that he was willing to appear a little more intimately in the affair than he really was. At any rate, he was willing to magnify Leggett to her, and he said: "If Leggett could see his way to using all the evidence he has——" He paused a moment, dandling a ruler deliberatively.

Isabelle colored slightly, to Nidstrom's surprise, and her eyes were even more wistful. "Yes," she murmured, with a little confusion; "he doesn't intend to use that?"

Nidstrom's mind was alert enough so that he covered his surprise as a wholly new and much more dramatic aspect of the case opened to him. Apparently she knew of the affidavit.

"He hasn't seen his way to using it, I believe," said he. "I think he feels bound not to."

"He won't use it even if it will save him?" she said, though Nidstrom could see that it was mostly just by way of hearing herself assured, of hearing him praised.

It was pretty enough in a way; but Nidstrom's mind was filled with the conception of something bigger, beside which the prettiness of the woman's sentiment seemed rather petty. He answered most sincerely, perhaps even a little harshly, looking straight into her eyes:

"I don't like Leggett in all respects. He has done some things that I have thought detestable. But if he had the most hopeless cause in the world he would face an army with it, and never bat an eyelash. There isn't an atom of the coward or shuffler or quibbler in him."

"I know that," Isabelle confessed, quickly and contritely.

She hesitated a moment; then asked, almost humbly: "This evidence—of course, it would make a good deal of difference?"

"As the thing stands, it might make all the difference between winning and losing," said Nidstrom.

It was some hours later that Isabelle threw aside the last of the futile attempts to write Leggett a letter, and instead wrote simply this:

"Can't you come up this evening? I must see you at once."

Finally, she could do nothing else than

THE MONEY CAPTAIN

merely to send that note. The letter, unless it said too much, said too little. What she felt that she must do was to put him back, in respect of this bribery evidence, to the position he occupied before their interview. She felt that she must blot out her intervention. It cut to the quick of her heart when she thought of the Deeres—but of all the people in the world, she should be the last to tie Leggett's hands in his extremity. It was finally an affair of law and government, and she must not attempt to judge it. Leggett must be right in that aspect of the matter. Of course, it made anything impossible between Leggett and herself—otherwise it would be as though she participated in the destruction of the Deeres. Anything further between Leggett and herself would in fact give her an effect of making her holiday in their ruin. Nothing remained but for her to step out once for all.

In the lump, that seemed not impossibly difficult; but in detail, especially as she thought it over hurriedly, going down to meet Leggett, it looked rather formidable.

She had let him be shown into the parlor, and it was evident that a state drawing-room would have better suited his attitude. He stood up and bowed, badly.

THE MONEY CAPTAIN

Perhaps in that first glance his very size, his thews and bulk, appealed to her by suggesting a daring, heroic capability that stood wounded before her. She perceived a sort of absurdity in his stiff attitude; yet she herself stopped midway in the room, not offering to shake hands nor asking him to sit down.

"I'm glad you came up," she said, abruptly, and she stepped to the back of a chair, on which she rested her hand. "I was wrong about that evidence," she hurried on, breathlessly. "I see that now. I didn't really understand it. It took me by surprise. I made a mistake to try to interfere. You must call all that as though it hadn't happened. That was what I wanted to tell you." She ended with a little nervous weakening of the voice, as with a person suffering from stage fright.

To Leggett, standing heavily at the side of the room, the sight of her face, the sound of her voice worked the old inevitable spell and evoked the frightful hunger with which he had been doggedly struggling ever since he first decided that he would ignore her note. He had no anger before her agitation, and he even appreciated the courage required to tell him that.

"I don't know that you made any mis-

THE MONEY CAPTAIN

take," he said. "I'm willing to say that you didn't. You needn't bother about it. Let it go." In a way he felt the situation to be rather pathetic.

"Oh, but I can't let it go!" Isabelle cried, quickly. She checked herself. Whatever else happened there should be no contest between them. She felt a reckless generosity in his attitude, and she shifted quickly to a more reasoned grasp of the situation.

"Come, sit down," she said, smiling a little, as though confessing to an absurdity in their thus standing stiffly apart. She pushed her chair forward. "Let's talk it over like sensible friends," she added.

At any rate, the interview should be on a rational, a civilized footing, rather than from that absurd pose. She smiled more brilliantly and directly, and, as though to begin all over, held out her hand.

At the touch of her fingers a constriction pained Leggett's heart, and he sat down in a moment of weakness.

"You must understand this," Isabelle began seriously. "I find I was quite wrong about that evidence. I ought not to have tried to judge. I see that I made a mistake. I know, after all, that I haven't a broad enough grasp on affairs of that kind."

THE MONEY CAPTAIN

She had thought out that point to make her surrender on, and she stuck to it, helplessly.

Leggett smiled a little at her reasoning. But the difficulties were by no means removed. He did not propose to seem to have forced her hand by getting arrested.

"What made you think it over that way?" he asked, with an effect of neighborly interest.

"Why, I just thought about it," Isabelle replied, with what she tried to make an appearance of candor, though her eyes barely met his and dropped again. "And the more I thought about it the more I saw that I'd made a mess. It—it isn't for me to judge. You must be free to do what you see to be best," she added, with a touch of hesitation which did not escape Leggett, and which went to confirm his idea that she yielded perforce.

"You've concluded that Deere ought to be punished?" he asked, mercilessly.

Isabelle drew a corner of her lip between her teeth, as she often did at a difficult place. "Oh, I don't know," she said abruptly, with a change of manner, with a direct appeal to him. "It is your fight. I ought not to be the one to tie your hands. I didn't realize it that way before. It's out of my reach—

only I don't want you to be—be at a disadvantage."

Leggett leaned back in his chair and looked over at her with an odd little one-sided smile that confessed much. "I didn't like having my hands tied—by you," he said, and then, as scrambling back to surer ground, "but maybe the case isn't so bad as you think. Dexter can do a good deal; but I have a fighting chance, even without that affidavit. I'm glad you thought it over again. But you have my promise, and you may keep it freely. I think I can win as it is. It's worth trying. I wouldn't mind thinking that I had given you that."

The moment she had spoken in that direct, appealing way, he had felt himself back on the friendly, confidential footing that had just preceded the rupture, and the hope which, in the intervening days' he had not only turned his back upon, but had spent much of his time buffeting and kicking, flowed strongly in upon him with a rising and intoxicating tide.

"Oh, but I couldn't let you!" Isabelle protested, a little startled and altogether overcome by that generosity. "If it should turn out wrong—think of that! Oh, I couldn't endure it. You can see that!" She leaned toward him, half frightened at the prospect which her words, and what she knew of his stubbornness conjured vividly up. "You must take back your promise. You must feel free to use the evidence."

To Leggett it was the Rubicon, and he crossed. He got up abruptly, and took the step that intervened between his chair and hers. "I don't want it," he said, peremptorily. "Why do you offer it back? I don't want the account squared. You know that I don't mind going to jail, or anything else—only you."

Isabelle's hands had been clasped on her knee as she bent toward him when he sat in the chair. She dared not move them now, nor her body. Her pose, from a spontaneous one, instantly became tensely rigid. She was afraid to stir. It was the plunge that she had so often dreaded, yet toward which, now that it was before her, she seemed to have been steadily and willfully moving all the time.

"You know that, don't you?" Leggett insisted, standing over her.

"Yes," she said, in a low voice, "I know that." His iteration restored her a little, and she leaned back in the chair, her hands idly in her lap, looking away from his face.

It was as difficult as it well could be for Leggett; but he tried again, with a final summoning of courage.

"See here, Isabelle," he began, with unwonted gentleness, "you know me pretty well. You know there are a lot of things I don't care so much about. I suppose I'm more or less reckless. But you—it's like having enough air to breathe. Won't you tell me now, at once—don't you care?"

The quality in him that she feared, the things she dreaded, were by no means explained away or lessened; but Fate had come up to the door. Her courage mounted over those things. She looked up and quickly put her hand into the big hand that hung with a kind of pathetic helplessness at Leggett's right side. "Yes, I care, Hamilton," she said, as candidly as he could have wished.

She felt rather than saw a premonitory limpness, and she knew that he was going to drop on his knees beside her chair. Her hand suddenly tightened its grip of his, and he felt its restraint.

"I care," she repeated, and as though to show him that she would make it irrevocable, she bent forward and kissed his hand before he could help it. "But there are a good many things to be considered," she added. "Bring your chair over."

Leggett obeyed meekly. In the score of seconds that elapsed while he stepped over and shoved his chair closer, it came to him as a kind of revelation that she had yielded, and his spirits soared triumphantly. He sat down and looked over at her, laughing boyishly.

"I don't see anything to consider," he said. "I've got a Prince Albert coat somewhere, and I can get the license in the morning. My Dexter case won't come before the grand jury until next week. Suppose we go down to St. Louis? Your gown is all right. We might go to New Orleans."

Isabelle smiled faintly at his enthusiasm. "You've already gone a good deal further than I have, haven't you?" she asked.

Leggett stared at her in an instant of consternation. "But of course you meant that," he said. "You meant that we should be married?"

It was so genuine that whatever provisional and probationary ideas she had indefinitely proposed to herself fell away and became trivial; even equivocal. "Yes," she said, "I meant that."

"Of course," he echoed, soaring again.

THE MONEY CAPTAIN

"Well, that's all there is to it, my dear. I know that we're both of age. We're both unattached. There's nobody to be asked."

"But then, there are the preparations, at least," she said.

Leggett sobered. "No," he said, quickly, "not any preparations, Isabelle. There's been a whole year of preparation. There's been thirty-two years of preparation on my side. I could never be as ready as I am right now. Everything might happen, you know."

He spoke with a kind of dismay, and Isabelle, who had begun with doubts about becoming engaged, found the whole question narrowed to whether the wedding should be in a week.

In spite of herself she had to laugh at him. "Why, you know we couldn't be married at once, like a couple of school children eloping," she said, still laughing at him. "It would be scandalous."

"Well," he assented, reluctantly. "Say a week from Sunday, then."

She laughed again. "But I have the saying," she replied. "Say sometime next May."

"Next May!" he repeated. He looked over at her silently, as though she had practiced a cruelty upon him. "That

THE MONEY CAPTAIN

sounds a long time," he said; then he added, abruptly, "Oh, not so long as that!" and he started forward as though he were going to leave his chair.

Isabelle put out her hand warningly. "You mustn't be absurd," she said warningly. "You must be reasonable," she added, more sweetly.

Leggett dropped back in his chair and looked over at her with his odd one-sided smile. "Well, I'll be reasonable," he promised. "Anything you like."

It had happened very swiftly and unexpectedly. Now Isabelle began to get her bearings in it, and she became very grave at once.

"The first thing," she said, "is this Dexter case. Of course—of course—you'll use that evidence now."

Leggett felt the quailing in her glance. He looked at her a moment, smiling a little. "Now, see here, Isabelle," he said, "let's be exactly square. You think a mighty lot of your Deeres."

"Of Anna and the children," she said.

"And you feel responsible for what I know—on account of what you told me."

"Well—it was awkward," she admitted, reluctantly, not looking at him.

"Of course," said Leggett. "Well, we'll

let it go. I have a fighting chance. Something will turn up. That will never be heard of again—especially not between us. Everything is to be left to me—including you. That's fair all around."

"But what will turn up?" she persisted.

"Oh, a lot of things," Leggett answered, easily. "I'm working on some things now. We'll just let the other be."

"Well—we might—for the present," she said, hesitatingly.

"Exactly—for the present," Leggett assented. He got up in spite of her and came over to her chair. "I don't ask for anything but just you," he said; then, in a helpless way, "You think—May?"

It sounded so helpless, so forlorn, that Isabelle threw herself to the other side of the chair, looking up and laughing, flashing her teeth and dimple at him—at this huge, helpless baby who asked for nothing but just her.

"Well, if nothing will satisfy you, say next week," she said, still laughing at him; and she slipped out of the chair before he could stoop and catch her.

CHAPTER XIX

In several ensuing days Nidstrom got his motive for resigning so bolstered up and padded out that it made a fairly presentable figure. Now that he had actually resigned Nell helped him with cheerful capability. They got to the point of speaking of the change as a stroke of good luck that had befallen, with some aid from themselves. Nidstrom renewed the correspondence more decisively with the abstract-of-title man. He bought three volumes of Michigan statutes, and a set of text-books on land titles and conveyances, bound in bright yellow law calf. The books filled a whole shelf in the library, and they looked so solid, so imposing, so like the actual body of the thing he dreamed of doing that his fancy hung affectionately around them. He got a secret joy out of merely looking at their backs. When he took down one of them to read in it, it put him in a kind of official frame of mind. While he went absently about his tasks at the Gas office, he was really sitting in his own office at High

THE MONEY CAPTAIN

Grove, Michigan, directing his own business —most successfully. He knew something about abstracting and conveyancing, and his imagination readily took hold of the details of the new business. The weather was splendid. Such bits of earth as he could get at in his paved ways steamed mildly with the promise of early spring. Even the grimy air of the city responded to the vernal hints. He saw a real estate agent about disposing of the house, and the agent, after marking down the price and marking up the commission, gave him hope of a speedy sale.

Meantime he had heard nothing from Dexter, so there was one more unpleasant bridge to cross. At times he regretted that he had left himself so entirely in the duke's hands. He might have made his resignation effective at a fixed date.

Early in the week following Mrs. Wilder's visit, as Nidstrom came into the ante-room at the Gas office, quite serene, the little electrical contrivance on the wall above the office boy's desk gave an angry buzzing, and the secretary's nerves leapt.

The tiny insistent machine responded to a button on Dexter's desk, and Nidstrom knew that the duke was back. The buzzing, like the imperious voice of the master,

THE MONEY CAPTAIN

filled not only the ante-room but the secretary's whole atmosphere. He gave a quick, apprehensive glance after the office boy as the tall youth ran to answer the summons; then he went hurriedly to his own room and shut the door as a kind of momentary barrier against that iron and direct mind to which he fancied he should soon have to give a clearer explanation of his resignation.

He could not help a somewhat bad conscience in respect of Dexter. Undeniably he had shuffled; he had not been frank; he had merely sneaked out, and before the dominating reintrusion of the duke's personality, he could not help feeling himself a rather small and slippery thing; he could not help feeling a little mean and apologetical.

However, the minutes passed. The machine buzzed and was still for long stretches and buzzed again. Visitors came and were admitted, sometimes, after a wait. Nidstrom went out to lunch and came back and worked far into the afternoon, apparently quite forgotten of the duke. Well, he was telling himself, somewhat defiantly, if Dexter didn't want to see him he needn't. Certainly he was willing to let the matter stand as it was.

It was after five o'clock when the office

THE MONEY CAPTAIN

boy came to his door and said, merely, "Mr. Dexter."

Nidstrom got up quickly, and was even a little grateful to Dexter for having remembered him.

The duke had on a new suit of lighter color and of more trig and jaunty effect than was common in his apparel. He even wore a red and white checked shirt and a small bow tie of a modest red. A gray, black-banded felt hat was pushed to the back of his bristling head. In a way, that rather modish and jaunty garb made him look older. Nidstrom noticed the white threads in his beard and the wrinkles at the corners of his eyes. The duke nodded to Nidstrom with the usual sufficient nod, and the secretary settled into the chair at the end of the desk, abeyant. Almost invariably his interviews with Dexter were over and through one or a half dozen processes of business that were going forward while the duke gave instructions or listened to his reports. Now, however, the desk was cleared into little systematic heaps of letters and documents and like litter, as though the day's work were done, and Dexter, facing him squarely and singly, slid forward in his chair and thrust his hands into his trousers' pockets.

THE MONEY CAPTAIN

"I got your letter, Mr. Nidstrom," he said, simply. "I was sorry to hear that you were thinking of leaving us."

"Well, I'm sorry to go in a way," said Nidstrom sincerely. "In many ways this position has been a very pleasant one. I've always been treated fairly."

"What's your idea in leaving?" Dexter asked, gravely.

"I have a good opportunity to get into a little business of my own—a set of abstract books—in the country. I've long thought of something like that. In fact, I had it all nicely fixed up in my mind before Drouillard failed. Of course, that upset things; but it seems to have worked around all right."

Dexter smiled a little with him at the joke of having lost his money through Drouillard.

"I like the country, anyway," Nidstrom went on. "Of course, there are bigger prizes in the city; but it's only one man in a million that can win them."

"Did you ever live in the country?" Dexter asked.

"No, not to live there really," Nidstrom admitted.

Dexter smiled over at the younger man thoughtfully. "It's quiet there," he said. "I used to think that when I got $100,000

THE MONEY CAPTAIN

I'd go into the country and live half the year anyway."

"Why didn't you?" Nidstrom asked quickly, smiling.

Dexter thought a moment, as though he were rehearsing the reasons and events in his mind for the interest he had in the retrospect rather than to find an answer to Nidstrom's question.

"Oh, I couldn't," he replied, simply. He pulled his hands from his pockets and clasped them back of his head, crumpling his hat, as though he had taken a deeper interest in the subject. "No man can," he added; "at least very few men can. A hundred thousand dollars, made as I've made my money and as most men make their money, means a hundred thousand new ties, a hundred thousand new things to do. So it goes, piling up. The more money I make the tighter I'm tied up. I've often wondered at the stupid idea people have of those things. The newspapers and sometimes political speakers talk about my making a million dollars or ten million as though it was a great big chunk of money that I'd dug up out of the cellar some way, and as though that was all there was to it—just finding the money and carrying it away. They talk about Dexter's gold. Why, I've got no

THE MONEY CAPTAIN

gold. I've got no money except just what I spend from day to day. I've got a great industry, a great enterprise that would be worth possibly a few hundred thousand dollars as junk if somebody didn't keep it going all the time, keep building it up. It's like a man with a great idea in his head. It don't amount to anything unless he can work it out, make it practicable, set it going, and when he does that he's got to give a million dollars to other people for every thousand that he can keep for himself—yes, more than that. I claim to have built up the Gas industry in this city as it stands to-day. Last year these companies took in seven and a half million dollars. I'd be well satisfied so far as mere money goes to be guaranteed for myself and my heirs one per cent of that amount clear and free, to know that I'd have that much without ever having to bother or think about business affairs. So far as the mere money goes, it's a failure. But you want your ideas to win. You want your plans carried out. You think you see opportunities that other people overlook, and you want to seize them and show that you were right. I get half sick of it sometimes," he added, coming back abruptly to the more personal affair. "I suppose I'd get altogether sick of it if I didn't have so much to do; so many things to carry through. You don't want to let anybody think he's beaten you. That's the way you get tied up in it. Good Lord! I wouldn't even dare stop to die now."

"Why not stop to live?" Nidstrom suggested.

Dexter gave his head a shake, decisively. "But if I did," he added, "I don't know what I'd do with myself. A man's got to do something, and his habits get settled."

The confidence, something like a confession, touched Nidstrom's sympathy. "You ought to take a long vacation, anyway," he suggested.

"I shall this summer," said Dexter. "My doctor has been advising me to—but my doctor is always advising me to do something. Good Lord!" he exclaimed, as though it touched his resentment, "a man's got to keep the business going. Nobody seems to appreciate that. Anyway, the man himself doesn't amount to so much. I suppose these Gas works would go on if I stopped. But I'm going away for four or five months pretty soon. That's one reason why I'm sorry to have you leave."

"Oh, well, the time of my going isn't of so much importance," Nidstrom made haste to say. "Of course, if it would make any

THE MONEY CAPTAIN

difference to you personally I could arrange to put it off till fall—at least I think I could."

"You've made your plans," Dexter replied. "I'll take it up soon. You've been a valuable man to me, Nidstrom. I appreciate that."

"Very good of you to say so," Nidstrom murmured.

"I'll take the matter up in a day or so," said Dexter, finally, "and see what we can do about a successor."

"Very well. Take your own time," said Nidstrom, and as Dexter made no further sign he got up.

"I hope you won't make any mistake—going to the country," Dexter added.

"Well, I hope not," Nidstrom replied.

Dexter reached up and laid hold of the rolling top of his desk as though to close it. His eye lingered a moment over the papers arranged in their systematic piles. "You go in debt some?" he suggested.

Coming from Dexter and applying to his own petty affairs the question was, of course, not offensive. "Yes, some," Nidstrom admitted.

Dexter smiled at him frankly. "Well, we'll see in a few days," he said. He plucked a folded sheet of paper from a pile on the desk, and rung for the office boy, and

THE MONEY CAPTAIN

Nidstrom knew that although it was six o'clock the duke had fallen back into that huge, endless coil of plans and schemes which he wove constantly and which enmeshed his life.

Nidstrom went out under the imperious influence of that power which Dexter imposed upon all minds that came directly into his presence. At that moment even High Grove, Michigan, appeared a little petty and shabby and futile.

He supposed that Dexter would tell him when he got ready to accept the resignation. But a week passed, in which his business with the duke went on just as though no resignation had been spoken of. Then, one morning at the house the postman brought him a letter with the Gas company's card in the corner of the envelope, which was superscribed in the duke's own hand.

The letter read:

"I find I can appoint your successor about the end of the month. I hope it will be no serious inconvenience to you to stay with us until that time. About that time I wish you would write me, as president of the company, a letter of resignation, to take effect the first. This letter will be for the purpose of keeping a record. I can say to you now that in consideration of your faithful

THE MONEY CAPTAIN

services in the last ten years I had decided to raise your salary this spring. Your going away, of course, puts it out of my power to pay you in that way, and what I enclose is simply in the nature of squaring accounts between you and the company to the end of this month. I don't know that this company ever paid out any money that it got better value for. If you should ever decide to return to Chicago we shall be glad to consider your application for a position. Personally, I wish you success and happiness."

The letter was signed by Dexter personally; but the check for $5,000 which was enclosed was the check of the Gas company, drawn by the treasurer of the corporation. Even at the first astonished glance, Nidstrom saw the machinery of the thing plainly enough. Dexter ordered the money paid, the disbursement to be duly approved and fitted into the neat mosaic of the corporation's accounts at any later date when it became convenient.

He went back to the dining-room where Nell was, and handed over the letter silently, just because he had nothing to say about it. When she had wonderingly read the letter, he handed over the check in the same way.

THE MONEY CAPTAIN

First of all it touched the woman's emotion. "It's fine and generous of him," she declared, in a little glow of gratitude; "generous, I mean, to acknowledge his obligation to you that way," she corrected.

"But, good heavens! I don't see how I can keep it," Nidstrom broke in despairingly.

"Not keep it! Why?" Nell demanded.

"Why, I don't know that he had any right to pay it to me," said Nidstrom, fumbling helplessly at the objection which was trying to take definite form in his mind. "We had a bargain. They paid me all they agreed to, and that ended it." He could not say in a word why the thing was so repugnant to him, why it savored both of charity and bribery.

"But you don't mean to say that you have to look out for a $25,000,000 Gas company, and see that it doesn't spend its money extravagantly," said Nell, "even supposing this was extravagant; and you know they could afford to pay you twice as much."

"No, it isn't that," Nidstrom fumbled again. "Suppose, in this matter of Leggett's, I should be called on to testify about going to Deere's office?"

"Of course you would testify then," Nell returned, promptly. "Mr. Dexter wouldn't expect anything else. It isn't right to throw money away, Victor," she added, gravely.

Nidstrom could not argue the point. It was not a matter of argument. The flavor of alms and of being bought was strong and offensive in his nostrils. It was, after all, a little piece of the loot tossed over to him to make him more surely one of the looting crew. But he could find no arguments, and it was in a way Nell's money and the child's which he proposed to throw away. He put the letter with the check in it in a corner of the drawer in the library desk, and he could not have said whether he had accepted it or rejected it. At moments he even felt resentful toward Dexter for having put upon him the necessity of deciding so painful a question.

When, the second day after, he was subpœnaed to appear and testify at Leggett's trial the following week, the question, in becoming acute, became momentous beyond the mere sum of money involved. He felt it in a way a turning point, a meeting of two widely diverging ways. That he should testify to having gone from Dexter's house to Deere's office the night of the council meeting was a matter of course from every point of view, since, evidently, some spy

THE MONEY CAPTAIN

had seen that much. But the whole matter of his going to Deere was exactly of that kind that it could amount to little or to very much, accordingly as he escaped with grudging answers to such interrogatories as were propounded to him on the witness stand, or as he let a full light upon the events and their environment. To tell all—the unusual summons to Dexter's house, implying a highly confidential and important character in the errand; the scene at Deere's office, with its furtive effect; Simpson's presence there; the figure that slunk into the shadow and emerged again, recognized afterward on the floor of the council as Alderman O'Toole—this would have a powerful, a fairly convincing effect.

Nidstrom felt in himself, as a sick spot in his conscience, an effect of having long temporized with certain iniquities and abominations; of having been in a provisional way of the propaganda of corruption and conscienceless greed; and at times his imagination flamed up with sacrificial fire over the thought of standing boldly out upon this trial and of giving all that he could to righteousness; of making a cleansing and baptismal plunge so that from that time forth he should know and others should know on which side he stood. The actual

THE MONEY CAPTAIN

difference in what he should say might not be so very great, as the chances of lawsuits and inalert lawyers went. But the difference in the spirit in which the thing was done would be great, and to do it in the right way involved as a matter of course the return of Dexter's check.

That meant the throwing away of Nell's money. He wondered whether his conscience in any event was worth so much money—as consciences and money counted in the affair of living. When Saturday night came he had not made his choice.

CHAPTER XX

On Sunday morning, about the hour when orderly people are thinking of church, Leggett walked around the front room in the small and high suite at the family hotel. The two front windows, at the altitude of the seventh story, overlooked a long and broad expanse of park, still in the dull coloring of winter. The limbs of the trees were bare, and near by the strong sunshine seemed to dissolve as it fell upon the wet, dun ground. To the south were the huge scars and excrescences left by the World's Fair. To the east the lake shone with a hard brilliance under the full sunlight.

Leggett looked calmly from the window a few moments; then he turned back to the room and began walking slowly about, with the effect of a big well-fed cat awake and discursively content in the limits of the chimney corner. It was not a large room, yet of comfortable size for one or two persons. Its furnishings suggested the hotel. A large leather couch took up one corner. A woman's cape—a trumpery little affair of velvet edged with fur—lay on the head of the couch, and a woman's hat, of the same sort of golden brownish velvet as the cape, lay by it, and a pair of woman's gloves lay on the hat. Leggett stood beside them, and looked down at them, his hands in his pockets, as though he were in the bodily presence of the consummation of an enormous joke.

The door to the inner room was not quite closed, and from that direction came a faint sound of splashing water. Leggett spent several motionless moments intently listening and following the dripping and splashing sounds up to the souse with which a person emerges from a bath-tub. Then he began walking softly around the room again.

Against the opposite wall stood a trunk, the cover thrown back with an effect of haste and disarray. Leggett went over to it and pulled up one of the green plush chairs with serene deliberation, and began looking at the things in the tray of the trunk, not lifting them, but stirring them with his big forefinger. His face relaxed only a little now and then, but he suggested being so nearly full of amusement anyhow that at each little accession he had to stop and let his merriment silently run over. In one of the compartments he found a small cut-glass jar, silver topped, with some pinkish powder and a piece of chamois skin in it, and that seemed to amuse him more than anything else. He did not move it, but, as though it were a kind of feat of legerdemain, he pried off the cover very carefully and took it up and looked it over, grinning a little. Some manicuring instruments held his discursive and satisfied attention for a moment, and he took up a little pile of handkerchiefs and smelled of two or three of them separately—all as though he were taking a deliberately greedy possession of the items of an estate which he had already acquired in the lump. A woman's mackintosh hung against the door, and he went over to it and looked for pockets in it. Then he sauntered to the window and stood, now glancing off at the lake and now looking back into the room, equally with an air of deliberate, idling content.

The door to the inner room opened quickly, and Isabelle came out, smiling brilliantly as soon as she saw him, as though in a way she too felt it a kind of tremendous joke. She wore the simple brownish street dress—so close-fitting that it moulded her fine figure statue-like—in which she had been married the evening before.

Leggett went over quickly and took her

in his arms. In a moment, after two ineffectual attempts, laughing and pushing against his breast with her hands, she got free.

"We're just old married people now, you know," she said.

"Oh, of course," he replied, "it's just narrowed down to you, so I must make the most of what's left to me." He led her over to the window and sat down and pulled her down to his knee. "We'll have some breakfast," he said, "as soon as I assure myself that you're not going away to-day."

"Did I keep you waiting long?" she asked.

"Just long enough for me to look over all your things," he replied, calmly.

"My things!"

"Certainly. I've been through your trunk. They're mine now, you know, and I wanted to see what sort of bargain I made. I hope you've got more gloves than those two pair, and more powder than that little bit."

Isabelle looked over to the trunk, then at Leggett. "You're welcome to all you can get of me in that trunk," she said. "My real armory hasn't been sent down yet. You know, there isn't a closet anywhere around here."

"Never mind the closets. Hang things

on the wall. Nobody's ever coming in here but just you and me—possibly a bailiff some day."

Leggett spoke jokingly; but the word reminded Isabelle of something grave. "That's Wednesday, then?" she said, meaning the trial on Dexter's charge of criminal libel.

Leggett nodded, looking up at her good-humoredly, as though it were an incidental matter of business. He had not satisfied her in respect of the course he intended pursuing, and, now, she turned to face him, and laid her hands on his shoulders as though she did not intend to be put off any longer.

"Don't you think you ought to publish that affidavit now?" she said earnestly.

"Oh, I don't know," Leggett answered, easily.

"But, Hamilton," she persisted, "it's only three days off. You ought to be prepared. Don't tease me any more. Tell me what you are going to do."

He still smiled slightly, as though he enjoyed her earnestness. "Well, you see, if I publish that affidavit I'll be giving away my advantage, won't I? As soon as I use that affidavit the thing will become pretty commonplace, as between you and me. I'll have to come down from my attitude of superiority as regards you. Don't you see?"

THE MONEY CAPTAIN

"Me?" Isabelle exclaimed. "But you mustn't think of me! Really, it's serious, dear; more serious than you think, I'm afraid. Put me out of your mind. Think of Dexter, with his money and influence and bad will to you!"

"Dexter!" Leggett laughed outright. "Why, Dexter be blowed! What do I care about Dexter? What can Dexter do to me? What can anybody else do to me? I've eaten the whole world, don't you see, and I'm now contentedly licking my fingers." He swept out his arm and crushed her against him.

"But then, you see," she said, in a moment, against the lapel of his coat, "if it hurts you it hurts me now. It's partly me, isn't it? And I don't propose to be hurt."

"Well, we'll see," he replied, lightly. "Of course, I can use this affidavit—if it seems necessary. Maybe your affidavit isn't so important as you think, after all. I'm pretty sure to get a good point out of Nidstrom. I don't think he knows very much; but he's one of those abnormal persons with a conscience, which is a sort of vermiform appendix—good for nothing but to get seeds in. That argues well for his giving up all that he does know. And I'm giving Polka Dot Simpson and his boys a good run for their money nowadays. I've put some people after 'em and they know it. They're all standing on the corner looking sullen and saying, 'We ain't done nothing.' If I can keep 'em worried enough somebody's likely to break away and confess. You see, I've got more than a seven spot in my hand besides your little affidavit. It isn't a bad chance as it stands."

"No!" Isabelle persisted, "you mustn't take the chances even if they are in your favor." She straightened up and looked earnestly in his face. "I want you to promise me to use that affidavit. Don't you see that I couldn't endure it if you didn't? It would be my fault. Come, now, promise me."

He looked quizzically and good-humoredly into her earnest face a moment. "Well," he said, amiably, "anything you like; whatever you wish."

"I knew you couldn't refuse, when you thought of it," she declared.

"Oh, thought!" he retorted. "Thinking has nothing to do with it. I don't propose to think for a week. I couldn't if I wanted to. It's just a question of dimples, of two brown eyes, of some plump, celestial curves. Shall we go down to breakfast or have some sent up here?"

CHAPTER XXI

It was true that the subterranean activities of which Leggett spoke disturbed Mr. Polka Dot Simpson's atmosphere and injured his peace of mind.

At the rear of the Polka Dot was a small and dingy room, its one window, screened with a piece of muslin, looking upon the forbidding alley; its door facing a row of dingy stalls designated "wine-rooms," and accessible from the "ladies' entrance." To this apartment Simpson was perpetually leading the way, doggedly, to listen to complaints and remonstrances—often, depending upon the state of the protestant with regard to liquor, to profane animadversions on his own intelligence and probity.

"Stop it?" he would repeat, irritably; "Good God! What I got to stop it with? What's the matter with you fellows anyhow? You come chasin' yourselves down here scared out of your wits because a dinky little one-cent newspaper's makin' faces at you. A man'd think you was a young lady's bible class and'd seen a mouse. What the

THE MONEY CAPTAIN

'ell can I do about it anyhow? If Dexter wants to send an editor to the pen, won't he do it? Go see Dexter yourselves if you want anybody to see him. Tell him yourselves to let up on Leggett. I ain't doing anything."

But the remonstrances continued, first to the ruin of Simpson's temper, and finally to the prejudice of his relatively temperate habit.

Standing behind the corner of his bar with his partner, who gave personal supervision to the varied industries of the Polka Dot, Simpson saw two well-known forms approaching the door. He looked up at the partner, solemnly, as calling him to witness a final stroke of Fate.

"O'Toole, too! I'm damned if it ain't O'Toole!" he exclaimed. He put down the glass and glowered along the top of the bar at the front door. "Now, that's just right," he said, impersonally; "make it unanimous. Let all hands come and rig the ship on old Simp. Tell him your troubles and ask him to help you out. He ain't got nothing better to do. Pitch into him; give him hell; he likes it. Come one, come all—all you moth-eaten, lousy stiffs from Stiffville. Come tell Simp there's a reporter rubberin' around and you're scared to death. He'll sympathize with you—you sweet-scented

THE MONEY CAPTAIN

skates"—the last words in a muttered undertone, immediately followed by, "Hullo, Pat!" to Alderman O'Toole, who had advanced down the room and at length found the host.

Simpson put out his hand hospitably, and the fat-bellied bottle, with a marble in a little wire cage over the mouth, was set out on the bar.

In a moment Mr. Simpson led the way to the inevitable back room. Not long afterward one of the Polka Dot's patrons, bareheaded and in a red wrapper, picking her way along the alley from an adjacent back door, paused by the curtained window—a ripe critic—and listened to the copious and varied profanity wherewith Simpson addressed his guests.

"Go see Dexter!" he exclaimed. "Why the devil should I see him? Go see him yourself. What if Dexter is fightin' Leggett. Let Leggett do his damndest and be damned to him. If Dexter sends him to Joliet everybody'll be bully good and rid of him. 'Tain't our funeral, is it?"

As Mr. Simpson thus delivered himself, glowering, he walked over and rung the bell for more drinks—although experienced Alderman O'Toole could easily see that he had taken too many. But Alderman

THE MONEY CAPTAIN

O'Toole interposed no objection, knowing that liquor is a fine help to some arguments.

Some two hours later Nidstrom, stepping to a filing case in the ante-room, encountered the wandering glance of Mr. Polka Dot Simpson, who sat in a chair next the window, his hat tilted to the back of his head, evidently waiting to be admitted to Dexter's room.

It was not an agreeable encounter. Nidstrom looked away hastily, but not so quickly as to escape a signal of defiance in the ex-alderman's eye. The encounter sharpened those apprehensions which had not been dull before. With the approach of the hour of Leggett's trial, Nidstrom's uncertainties multiplied. His mind perspired doubts. All his perceptions of the affair verged to a question mark. He could not help feeling Dexter as a kind of huge inhuman mass weighing upon him and pressing him to the moment of decision. Sitting in the duke's room toward noon his eyes had shifted often to that black-framed face, with so sharp a conception of the man's activities that it was as though they had suddenly been dramatized before him.

Upon how many men was that bold, greedy will then pressing inexorably?

In another time, the secretary thought, its

THE MONEY CAPTAIN

violence would have been legibly translated in violent acts. With a sword in his hand Dexter would have been an easily cognizable figure. The bribe that he carried instead confused his outlines so that it troubled one to say in how far he exceeded the law.

To announce the fact! To define the outlines! To disclose Dexter with distinctness for what he was! For a moment it seemed a heroic, a necessary office. Then the duke's calm face, his even voice as he sat at the desk going over the details of business, passively alleged an hysterical absurdity in the idea. It was hard to gainsay that serene, assured air. Nidstrom saw himself, at the end of the denunciation, shrinking under the calm tones of the duke's voice which said, "Why, this poor young man is crazy!" What could overcome that superlative confidence? He supposed that Dexter had sent for Simpson, and the very fact of the ex-alderman sitting composedly in the ante-room only a few hours before the time of Leggett's trial heightened the secretary's idea of Dexter's supreme, flawless assurance. Who else would have dared do that?

In fact, however, Nidstrom made this devoir to Dexter's courage without grounds. When, finally, yielding to intolerable pres-

THE MONEY CAPTAIN

sure, Simpson agreed to see Dexter and try to stop the prosecution of Leggett, which promised to bring disastrous reprisals upon some of his friends, he was in that state of mind when considerations of prudence had little weight —owing somewhat to irritation, but more to the reckless inspiration of the fat bottle.

According to the etiquette of the situation he should have been in a state of polite ignorance as to Dexter's existence, and any petition should have been presented to Deere, whom alone he was supposed to know. At least, he should have arranged privately for an interview with Dexter. But the time was short, this being Tuesday, and Leggett's trial being set for Wednesday. And an attempt at prearrangement might be Dexter's opportunity for evading him altogether. He took some more drinks, therefore, and went boldly to headquarters.

When the office boy carried in his name, Dexter was about to lay the slip of paper with two others on his desk and to consider receiving the caller at his leisure. But it chanced that his eye caught the name, and the motion of his hand toward the desk was arrested as he looked thoughtfully at the card. The boy waited. A bare instant of deliberation elapsed. Then Dexter dropped

THE MONEY CAPTAIN

the slip of paper to the desk, and went on dictating to the young woman who sat at the corner of the long table.

The temper of provisional defiance in which Simpson came to the office did not improve with time. Two men whom he knew and three who were strangers to him came in at intervals, waited, and were admitted to the inner room and went away. The electric buzzer called a dozen times. Each time the office boy emerged from the duke's room and went about some errand without looking at Simpson. There were moments when it seemed to the ex-alderman not only permissible but obligatory to walk into Dexter's presence unannounced, curse the duke roundly and walk away—but there were those several figures waiting for a report of the success of his mission. He slid down in the chair and pulled his Derby hat to his eyebrows, and regarded this monstrously insulting demesne of the duke with sidelong sullen glances.

Four o'clock came, Simpson having waited an hour and a half. Whatever secret misgivings he had been possessed of in respect of its being just the square thing to come down on Dexter in his office this way, had wholly dissolved. His attitude of resentment toward the forces which had

THE MONEY CAPTAIN

impelled him to come had long since disappeared. In the light of Dexter's insulting treatment, his friends became not merely tolerable, but acceptable. What was this rotten duke thinking about to keep him out there that way! Anyhow, when he did get in, the interview would not be a pleasant one.

Abruptly, he got up and walked from the office. Some impossible but destructive schemes were boiling in his mind. Below, in the first saloon that he came to, he even grated his teeth loudly two or three times. His idea was to send Dexter an ultimatum, as an ultimatum might be interpreted in the Polka Dot. He went into a stall in the saloon and called for a drink of approved potency. He even got out a notebook and pencil and attempted to consider the composition of an ultimatum. But, aside from the difficulties of composition, enormously heightened by the gin cocktail, the very sight of the writing materials warned him. Things written and signed were always to be avoided. And there was that pig Dexter, as it were, just at his hand, and refusing to see him! He even wept a little as he cursed and grated his teeth.

It was a quarter of five when he reappeared in the ante-room of the Gas office. He walked with deliberation, but quite steadily, to the little desk and leaned his hands on it and looked at the office boy with eyes that squinted a little through the intentness of the gaze.

"I want you to tell Mr. Dexter that I'm waiting for 'im," he said, with careful enunciation.

The boy hesitated an instant. He noticed only that Simpson's breath reeked of liquor, but he supposed that was its normal state. He again wrote the name on a slip of paper, and carried it inside.

Simpson went to a chair, and placed himself in it with care, as though it were a sort of engineering feat. A quarter of an hour passed—a period that contained much actual danger for the duke.

Then the office boy, coming from the inner room, lifted an indicative forefinger. Simpson waited to relight the butt of his cigar; then he walked with deliberation into the inner room, his hat on the back of his head.

Dexter was reading a letter. He finished it, shoved it to one side, and laid a paperweight on it. Then he looked up at Simpson without speaking or even nodding. He smelt the whisky, but it was merely one small item in his general disgust.

Simpson, with the same deliberation, dis-

THE MONEY CAPTAIN

posed himself in the chair at the end of the desk.

"Can't you let up on this row with the *Eagle?*" he asked, steadily.

Dexter merely looked at him a moment, and asked, coolly, "What is it you want?"

"Why, this row with the *Eagle* is stirring up a lot of trouble, and the boys don't like it," said Simpson, with his careful enunciation, eyeing the other. "It's gettin' them into a bad box, and they don't feel like standin' for it. Leggett and his folks have been nosin' around. Probably somebody or other has told something, and some of the boys think there'll be a nasty mess made of it. Good God! you know there's always trouble enough in this business without any of us goin' out to look for it."

"I don't understand you," said Dexter, shortly. "Talk plainly, if you can. What do you mean by 'this business,' and 'some of us,' and 'the boys,' and whose business is it if I have a row, as you call it, with the *Eagle?* Talk up."

Simpson leaned forward, resting his forearms on the arms of the chair, and scowled into Dexter's face. "I mean you're raising hell with the *Eagle*, and that's stirrin' Leggett up to send out a lot of spies and maybe get what he calls some confessions and make a nasty muss in his newspaper about bribery 'n' corruption in connection with the Northwestern Gas ordinance. And you oughtn't to do it. As I said, there's always trouble enough without any of us going out to look for it. The boys don't like it, and they won't stand for it! You let up on Leggett and he'll let up on the boys. See?" He struck the corner of Dexter's desk with his fist.

Dexter stared hard at the figure before him. Then he gave a laugh which was simply one contemptuous and amused expulsion of breath. "Did the boys send you here?" he asked.

"Not exactly," Simpson replied. "Knowin' how they felt I came to prevent trouble."

"Well, you'll prevent trouble, Simpson, by going away again," said Dexter, calmly. "There's nothing more to say." He reached toward the row of electric buttons on the corner of his desk.

Simpson stretched out a forbidding hand. "Now, wait a minute," he said, loudly and roughly.

Dexter, in fact, did wait, eyeing the ex-alderman narrowly, his finger ready at the button.

"That won't do," Simpson went on, threateningly. "It ain't square, Dexter,

THE MONEY CAPTAIN

and you know it. We help you out and stand by you, and you've got to stand by us, or, by God! there'll be trouble."

"Don't threaten!" Dexter warned, in a rising voice.

"I will threaten!" Simpson retorted. "We're in the same boat, and we don't propose that you're goin' to scuttle the boat. We won't have it. Understand that!"

Dexter looked hard at the ex-alderman for a moment. "Get out of the office!" he said, abruptly.

"I won't get out!" Simpson declared, loudly.

"Get out, or I'll have you thrown out. You're drunk anyhow."

"You're a damned liar!"

"Get out!" Dexter stood up abruptly, menacingly.

With nearly simultaneous motions, Simpson rose—and struck out.

The vigorous blow fell hard on the left lapel of Dexter's coat, and Dexter doubled abruptly into his chair.

For a full instant, the duke remained motionless, as though bound to the chair—an unpleasant spectacle, his mouth open as, after an instant's obstruction, he took in a long, gasping breath. There was a contraction of the muscles in his brow and

THE MONEY CAPTAIN

around the corners of his eyes as with one in pain. His eyes were fixed frightfully on Simpson's face, all the rage in the momentarily helpless body finding vent through them. They glared with a kind of ferocity, and even in the first instant of bodily shock Dexter felt with keenness this monstrous, incredible thing—he, Dexter, had been struck by this drunken creature of the saloons and stews.

Simpson's mind, both sodden with drink and blurred with anger, took the measure of the situation but slowly and imperfectly. He stood over Dexter, scowling, his lower jaw protruding, ready to strike again. It was only when he saw Dexter make an ineffectual effort to rise from the chair that the dull and clumsy instrument of his perception began to adjust itself to the significance of that distorted, glaring face and helpless body. The conception of a serious mishap, a grave disarrangement, in the million-dollar piece of machinery before him—a disarrangement following his own blow—prompted Simpson characteristically. He turned on his heel and walked briskly from the room and from the Gas office. As he went, he thought with deep satisfaction, "I punched him one anyway, damn him!"

Once on the street, he made his way by

THE MONEY CAPTAIN

such short cuts and turnings as suggested themselves to his ingenuity to the house of a person whom he called a "lady friend." He had found the house convenient on two other occasions in his career as a vantage point from which to await developments without prejudice to whatever course of action the developments might seem to make expedient.

A mere hissing from Dexter's lips followed the retreating form of the ex-alderman. With all his power and resources, with all the vast costly machinery about him, that simple, pitiful sibilation was the only vehicle that his wrath could find. As soon as Simpson disappeared, the struggle ceased. Dexter's muscles relaxed, with a curious effect of settling down into an abyss. He stared dully ahead of him with a singular feeling of emptiness. There was still a pain in the region where the blow had fallen. After a moment he got his finger to the row of electric buttons.

The office boy entering found him sitting sidewise to the desk, his arm resting on it, and his head lying on his arm.

"Call a carriage," said Dexter, in a weak voice.

The boy slid from the room with frightened alacrity. In the ante-room he hastened to the telephone. Then he turned around helplessly, and entered Nidstrom's room.

"I dunno but Mr. Dexter's sick," he gasped. "I'm going to call a carriage. Maybe if you or Mr. Goddard 'd step in there——" He stared at Nidstrom in a frightened way.

Nidstrom got up hastily, in vague alarm. "What makes you think so?" he demanded.

"Well—he sort o' looked that way," the boy mumbled, half abashed. "He's got his head on the desk."

"Probably it's nothing," Nidstrom replied brusquely, although it was only his own alarm that made him disparage the boy's fright. "Call the carriage."

"Yes, sir," said the boy, meekly.

When the boy went out, Nidstrom in his turn stood hesitant. This portentous affair of the duke's illness was not a pleasant thing to have on one's hands. Mr. Goddard, the treasurer, red-bearded, hollow-eyed, dry, capable, like a staunch, somewhat musty old receptacle in which secrets are stored, occupied the room next to Nidstrom's. To him Nidstrom went. Mr. Goddard arose at once with his accustomed manner of dry, unvarying capability, whether it should be a question of certifying a voucher or wit-

THE MONEY CAPTAIN

nessing a death. Nidstrom followed the treasurer into the ante-room, but he stopped there.

Mr. Goddard found Dexter sitting upright in his chair, his head drooping forward, his eyes heavy. He glanced up as the treasurer came in.

"Shan't I call a doctor?" the treasurer asked abruptly, but with a softened voice.

"No," Dexter replied. "I'm all right. Let me know when the carriage comes."

Mr. Goddard observed an uncanny pallor in the duke's face, and a kind of heaviness and flabbiness, as though he had suddenly grown old; but it was the duke, there was no question about that, and when Dexter repeated, briefly, "I'm all right," Mr. Goddard had nothing to do but walk out.

The office boy went out to the curbing to watch for the carriage, summoned from a public stable; and up-stairs in the long suite of rooms among the chiefs of the duchy information of the duke's seizure was communicated with electrical swiftness and stillness.

When the office boy returned, instead of announcing the arrival of the carriage to Dexter, he again sought Nidstrom. He was still palpably frightened.

"The carriage 's here," he said.

THE MONEY CAPTAIN

It was on Nidstrom's tongue to say, "Tell Mr. Dexter"; but he thought better of it and went himself to Dexter's room. The duke had not moved since Goddard left.

"The carriage is waiting," said Nidstrom, with a softened voice, in his turn; then, "Shan't I go down with you?"

"No," said Dexter, briefly. He appeared to take their anxiety as a matter of course, and he showed no irritation. Nevertheless he waited a moment, after answering, before he essayed to rise. He got out of the chair somewhat slowly and stood by the desk, his hand on the edge of it. "You might hand me my coat," he said.

Nidstrom picked the light overcoat from the lounge, and put it over Dexter's arm, with a subtle sense of repugnance as when one lifts a man cripple. The duke walked slowly but steadily through the ante-room, down the hall to the elevator landing; and then, below, across the marble floor and the flagging outside to the carriage. He got the door open and stepped into the vehicle with the same effect of cautious ponderousness and sank down in a corner of the seat, the upper part of his overcoat clutched under his arm and its skirts spreading over the seat and over his knee. He knew the world outside the carriage window with as perfect a

THE MONEY CAPTAIN

consciousness as ever, and he knew, in the lump, this strange, impenetrable, deadly wall that had so suddenly risen up between his will and that world. He was not alarmed. At the very bottom of him was the living, dogged idea to keep very still and let this bar which had so suddenly imposed istelf upon his nerves and arteries slip away; to wait with his teeth shut until the thing passed by.

At home he dropped his hat and coat at the footman, rather than suffered him to take them, and went on, slowly, steadily to the great staircase. He climbed up, helping himself by the balustrade, as though that brief journey were a kind of epitome of his career in which nothing could daunt him or turn him.

The footman watched the retreating and mounting figure with a furtive curiosity. For some moments after Dexter had disappeared he waited, listening. But he heard no summons of any kind, and he turned on the electric lights, impassively. Then he went into the little reception room off from the hall, and regarded himself critically in the mirror.

When Miss West came in half an hour later, he mentioned that Mr. Dexter seemed not very well. The girl stopped only for

THE MONEY CAPTAIN

a hurried question, then ran hastily upstairs. She went first to that room with the business table in it. There was no light within.

"Uncle Archy! Uncle Archy!" she called, softly.

The words roused Dexter from a torpid napping. "Yes," he answered.

The girl came over to where he lay stretched on the couch, and she dropped on her knees beside him.

"Aren't you well?" she asked, and he felt the anxiety in her soft, rapid breathing.

"Oh, yes, I'm well enough," he replied, with an attempt at cheerfulness. "I'm well enough. Don't wait dinner."

She felt his hands and face. "I believe you've got a chill," she said. "I'm going to have Dr. Reynolds over."

"No, it isn't worth while," Dexter replied. "I'm all right. The doctor would bother me. I'm tired."

Dexter himself then felt no uneasiness. He had fallen into a kind of sleep soon after he laid down, and what he chiefly felt was an enormous capacity to rest. It seemed to him that if he should sleep a little while he would be quite right, and he even suspected that he had exaggerated the turn he got in the office.

THE MONEY CAPTAIN

His manner nearly reassured Miss West. "But it wouldn't do any harm," she said.

"It would bother me," he replied. "I'm just tired. I'll stay here a while, and then I'll be all right. If I want anything I'll ring."

He would not suffer her to take off his shoes. She got a pillow under his head, and, after some fond and ineffectual lingering, went out, closing the door so that he could be quiet. Twice in the early evening she went to the door and opened it stealthily and listened and tiptoed away. It was nearly 10 o'clock when she next approached the door. Listening a moment, before turning the knob, she heard a sound as though he had slid from the couch to the floor.

She flung open the door, calling, and started toward the dark side of the room, where the couch was. In a shadowy way she could see something moving. She called again, and turned back to the little iron key beside the door-casing that controlled the electric current. As she touched this the room sprang into light, and she saw Dexter, clutching the head of the couch, half raised from his knees, his face distorted, his eyes staring fiercely at her, his head with an appearance of being drawn between his shoulders like that of a pugnacious animal.

THE MONEY CAPTAIN

There was a hurrying of feet from different ways. An electrical air of agitation assailed the whole great house.

A footman and a maid reached the door at nearly the same instant. They saw Miss West and Dexter at the head of the couch. She was trying to lift him up. His great weight had borne her down to her knees, and they had an odd appearance of struggling with each other. The man quickly got the duke on the couch. He was then speechless. The butler and more maids came, all terrified and helpless. The butler ran to telephone for the doctor. In a moment it appeared that there was nothing more to do, and the group of servants stood near the door, alarmed, but inert and staring at the thick-set, black-bearded man stretched on the couch, speechless and breathing through his open mouth in long, laborious inspirations, and at the girl who knelt beside him, holding his hand in both hers, kissing it again and again, looking with agonized intentness into his empurpled, ugly face.

In time the doctor came, and sat by learnedly while the duke died.

CHAPTER XXII

At a quarter after eleven Leggett stood by the ancient table in his den at the *Eagle* office putting on his cuffs. He was going home, and he was not satisfied. The last directions had been given respecting the printing of the bribery disclosure in the morning's paper. The disclosure would, of course, be a neat counter-irritant to his own trial, which would begin at 10 o'clock in the morning. But, in view of Isabelle, Leggett would have preferred another way if one could have been found.

The soiled, nondescript jacket that he wore in the office lay on the table. He was getting into his coat when the city editor burst in, holding out a little sheet of yellow tissue paper. Leggett knew it instantly for a bulletin from the news bureau. He caught the sheet and spread it between his fingers. It said:

"Reported that Dexter died of apoplexy half an hour ago. Investigating."

Leggett started rapidly for the door, saying as he hastened: "Who you got out there? Who's on the south side. Have you telephoned?"

Nothing in the world counted now but the news. It was of no importance in the world whether Dexter was dead or alive. The only thing of importance was that the *Eagle* should know at once, with all possible copiousness of detail, which was the fact.

Leggett was thrusting a telephone directory into the hands of a young man. "Call up the residence. Find out whether he's dead and if he is, when he died and what he died of and who was there and who attended him. Then, as soon as you get what you can there, call up the residence of Dr. Edmund Reynolds, that's Dexter's physician, and find out what you can there—as, when the doctor was called, if he was called, and whether Dexter's been ailing lately; and if Dexter isn't dead, find out what his state of health has been lately. Go down, stairs and use the business office telephone so's to leave this one free. Thompson" (to another young man), "the street cars are quicker than a cab; go to the house as fast as you can. Ask for the physician, if Dexter is dead, and get all you can about how he died. After you've got the mere fact that he died, every detail is worth a million dollars. And if he is dead, everything will be torn up and demoralized around the house—there'll be no discipline, you know. Get hold of the servants, those that were in the room when he died or around him. Get down there quick, before they get organized again. And telephone us as soon as you leave the house. Maybe you can telephone from the house. It's late, remember." (To the city editor:) "Have somebody start right away getting up a biographical sketch. We've got his picture ready." For the first time the juxtaposition of certain events occurred sharply to him, and he grinned slightly.

He himself got a fresh proof of the cut, three columns wide, which was already lying on the imposing stone ready to be put into the front page of the paper, surrounded by the bribery disclosure. At the top and bottom of the cut were certain descriptive lines in heavy type. At the top of the proof, above the printed line, "Archibald Dexter, Arch Corruptionist," Leggett wrote, "Archibald Dexter, Builder of the City's Gas System." And at the bottom of the proof, below the printed lines, "This is the Man for Whose Benefit Simpson Tried to Bribe Alderman Bueloh," he wrote, "Died Last Night at His Magnificent Home on

THE MONEY CAPTAIN

Drexel Boulevard in the Prime of His Activity."

He handed the proof to the sub-foreman. "Have those new lines set up," he said; "but don't take down the old lines. We may have to use them." And Dexter's portrait, with its dual designations, waited on the imposing stone for the impartial election of the editor, according as the duke was dead or alive.

For two hours the establishment was given over to the epic stress of getting an adequate account of the death in the early edition. Bits of copy, snatched at by breathless men, rained in from various directions, and Leggett drove the bits as a merciless shepherd drives a flock of skurrying sheep, until the last grimy hand, reaching in through the tiny window of the copy-cutter's cage in the composing room, caught from the hook the last narrow strip with barely a dozen words on it.

In the lull in the storm which came with the sending down of the last form to be stereotyped for the early edition, Leggett went to his den. As he munched the roll and sipped the coffee which he had ordered brought in, the human aspects of the affair began to shape themselves to his mind. The death of Dexter began to take size and

THE MONEY CAPTAIN

color beyond a mere subject for copy. Whatever else might be thought of it, it was the sudden disappearance of a large edifice. Leggett felt himself, in a way, at an historic moment, and he rose to it. He recalled the editorial page for the late edition, and wrote a short article, barely two hundred words, in which he sought to express the feeling that Dexter was now an historic remains, to be regarded chiefly for its great value in illuminating its epoch.

The east was washing into dim opalescence and the streets gave the echoing, exaggerated noise of many early carts as Leggett's cab drew up at the hotel. His rooms were dark and the doors were locked. He tapped lightly, listening, and in an instant Isabelle's voice on the other side of the door asked guardedly, "Who is it?"

"Whom were you expecting?" Leggett replied.

He stepped in and turned on the electric light, and Isabelle, still warm and drowsy from the bed, holding one hand over her eyes because of the sudden light, and groping for him with the other, murmured, "What ever made you so late?"

"Dexter's dead," he replied, gravely.

The hand dropped, and Isabelle stared at him, her lips apart. "Dexter?" she gasped.

THE MONEY CAPTAIN

"Heart failure, they called it; all over in a minute. It happened at 10 o'clock."

Isabelle fixed him with a stare which gradually heightened to a grave, a solemn regard. In the wakeful intervals of the night, while she waited for him, anxious over his absence, the trial which was to begin in the morning was always close to her thoughts. It loomed over her when she started out of uncertain sleep. However her husband was armed and assured, it was a final, desperate life-and-death contest with the most formidable of antagonists; and even if he won there were the Deeres to be ruined. This sharp, ultimate aspect of the affair came again and again, and her heart quaked at every recurrence. But Dexter was dead!

The tragedy of that abrupt snatching away in the midst of his powers and splendors made its appeal to her. It had all the inevitable dreadfulness of the handwriting on the wall. No man dared say, "This is for my profit." Still, he was dead —and Leggett was alive, standing before her, whole, unscathed. The Deeres were spared.

All that she could have said, she expressed much better by putting out her arms and gathering him against her and putting her

THE MONEY CAPTAIN

head on his shoulder with a kind of solemn content.

Leggett put his arm over her shoulder. "Yes, we're alive," he said. And, in a moment, "To be dead! Pah!"

The *Eagle*, with an effect of funereal hysterics, contrived by enormous black type and exclamation marks, gave the Nidstroms the news of Dexter's death. To Victor there came at once the figure óf the duke, walking through the ante-room and down the hall to the elevator, already stricken but going to his last fight in a kind of admirable wholeness, as he had lived throughout. At the Gas office he found himself plunged into unexpected and exacting affairs by the death of the master of the machine. Goddard and Rose and Buford, the banker, spent most of the day conferring, and before noon it was made perfectly plain to La Salle Street—which was early inclined, optimistically, to view the duke's death as a pessimistic opportunity in respect of its effect on Gas shares—that, while the master hand was inert, there were some other hands ready to do what was needful. Gas shares declined only a couple of points, and quickly recovered.

Nidstrom put off thinking of his peculiar position at the Gas office until after dinner.

It appeared that no one at the office knew of his intended resignation.

"I shall tell Goddard just what happened," he said to Nell—"that is, after a while; in a few weeks, when things get back to a regular routine."

"You still think that you ought to leave?" Nell asked, quietly.

Nidstrom then knew, if he had ever pretended otherwise, that her acquiescence in his country scheme had been merely a result of loyalty and not of conviction.

"Why, I don't know," he said, dubiously. "Now that Dexter's gone, some way it looks different. He was so strong that he weighed on all of us, and he made all of us seem somehow like just little pieces of his bigness, so that whatever he did we seemed to be doing in a way, too. Now that he's gone it seems rather different. I know that I can do a lot of things up there that nobody else can—at least, nobody else can do them as well without a long apprenticeship. In a way, it's a kind of brutal thing to say, but the removal of Dexter's personality seems to give my individuality more show—you understand? I don't quite know how it is, but the idea of staying isn't repugnant to me now. I feel as though I was of some importance up there—and, well, so long as

THE MONEY CAPTAIN

Dexter was around nobody else could feel of any importance. He was the whole machine. Now the machine will be a lot of small pieces, and I suppose I can be one of the pieces."

"I'm sure you can," Nell replied, promptly and joyfully. "And you'd never have been really contented in the country, Victor. It's too small and quiet."

"Well," Nidstrom half assented, doubtfully. "Still, I don't know that I can stay now."

"Of course you can," said Nell, indignantly. "They couldn't get along without you."

"Well, I'd hate to dare 'em to try," said Nidstrom, indulgently, "and in a way I've been paid off," he added.

"No, you haven't," said Nell; "that was just to compound the increased salary they were going to give you. Well, you needn't ask for an increase of salary now."

Nidstrom troubled himself over it a while. "Oh, well," he confessed finally, "you never can get to any really satisfactory ground in those things—unless you go by the rule of what's business—and that rule is to keep as much as you can. I suppose it's business to keep this and call it a compounding of the raise of wages."

THE MONEY CAPTAIN

"What does it amount to to Dexter, anyway—I mean if he were alive?" was Nell's final word.

"Well, I suppose Miss West won't need the $5,000," Victor admitted.

"Miss West? Does she get it all?" Nell asked quickly, with a new interest.

"I understand most of it finally goes to her, after the widow is through living in her sanitariums," said Nidstrom.

All those millions! And Arthur—Nell began dreaming it over. Sometime later, when Nidstrom left her and Arthur in the library for a moment, she managed to say:

"Victor says that Miss West will be his heir."

Arthur smiled a little at the elaborately incidental way in which she said it. After Nell and Victor had gone up-stairs he sat long thinking it over, without rancor.

The duke's death had been the touch that lifted the girl definitely out of his slight and half-ironical illusion. It was like a coronation that fixed her firmly in a great sphere, much beyond his reach. In a way it was fine and beautiful—all that huge accumulation of pillage coming to the white, firm hands of this pretty, amiable, capable, good-hearted young woman. The sudden substitution of her graceful and gracious figure for

THE MONEY CAPTAIN

the swart and iron figure of the duke was like an apt transformation scene, prophetic of the future. Arthur saw her, dignified and broadened by the new station, taking command of the great house and putting her influence into the great machine down-town, womanly, but competent. In its way it was a great station.

It came back to him how she had sat beside him in the street car, the edge of her little cape brushing his shoulder. He looked around the little room in which he sat, homely, cozy, kindly; and it occurred to him that as the death of Dexter expunged from his fortune that color of greedy vulgarity and left its gold untarnished, it also made a vastly wider difference between that station on Drexel Boulevard and this on Tremont Avenue. Dexter, for all his success, was a figure in the common democratic foreground of business; he was intimately and solely of the great everyday warp and woof of toil. He bore all his fruit at once —when he died. An heirship was required to give the fortune value.

"After all," he thought, "this duke was only the miller. Somebody else must eat the bread."

THE END

www.ingramcontent.com/pod-product-compliance
Lightning Source LLC
Chambersburg PA
CBHW030738230426
43667CB00007B/760